bonnie stern's essentials of home cooking

Bonnie Stern's

essentials of home cooking

random house canada

NATIONAL LIBRARY OF CANADA CATALOGUING IN PUBLICATION

Stern, Bonnie
        Bonnie Stern's essentials of home cooking

Includes index.
ISBN 0-679-31254-4

1. Cookery. I. Title.

TX714.S85 2003   641.5   C2003-902367-2

Project Editor	Shelley Tanaka
Photography	Robert Wigington*
Food Styling	Olga Truchan, Wendy Bowen
Prop Styling	Sue Florian
Photo Assistant	Mark Paré

Excluding page 180 (Digital Vision)

The following suppliers were particularly generous in lending props used in the food photography:

Elle Maison, Toronto
Williams-Sonoma, Toronto
Pottery Barn, Toronto
Villeroy & Boch, Cookstown, ON
Rob McIntosh China, Woodbridge, ON

Printed and bound in Canada

10 9 8 7 6 5 4 3 2 1

For my family, more essential to me than anything else—Mark (who loves my risotto), Anna (lemon pavlova), Fara (caramelized onion pizza) and Ray (anything you make, Bonnie, is perfect, but an apple dessert would be nice).

Contents

Acknowledgments

The older I get, the more people I have to thank. I am so lucky to be able to work at what I love and to have the support of my family, friends and colleagues.

Since I began my cooking school in 1973, I have taught more than three thousand classes. It is like having a focus group every night, and I am so grateful to my students who tell me what they like to eat and what they need to know to make a recipe work. There is no greater reward than people telling me that they can depend on my recipes and that they use them all the time. If they are successful, then I am successful.

Thanks to Random House Canada for welcoming me into their house and for having so much enthusiasm for this project. Everyone went way beyond the call of duty, notably Anne Collins, Tanya Trafford, Scott Richardson, Scott Sellers, Sarah Davies, Brad Martin and John Neale. Thanks to my friend and editor Shelley Tanaka, for putting up with me and especially for telling me when to stop changing things; to my friend and lawyer Marian Hebb, who tells me when to stop worrying; and to Robert Wigington, Olga Truchan, Wendy Bowen and Sue Florian for the delicious photographs that make my food look so good.

I am grateful to be a part of such a generous and professional food community—the suppliers who provide me with incredible ingredients, the chefs whose restaurants I love to go to and the extraordinary teachers who teach at my school, especially Giuliano Bugialli, Hugh Carpenter, Mitchell Davis, Madhur Jaffrey, Nick Malgieri, Jacques Pépin, Nina Simonds and Joanne Weir.

My thanks to my staff at the cooking school— especially to Rhonda Caplan for testing these recipes and to Anne Apps, Jenny Burke, Dely Balagtas, Lorraine Butler, Sadie Darby, Glen Gaston, Josée Kline, Letty Lastima, Maureen Lollar, Laura Mannion, Francine Menard, Mark Rupert and Linda Stephen for working so hard so that I could have the time to write this book.

Although writing and publishing a cookbook is a big job, it is only the beginning. Thanks to members of the media who have always been so enthusiastic about my recipes, the book buyers and booksellers who make room on their shelves, and everyone who buys my books when there are so many others to choose from. I hope these recipes will become part of your home cooking, too.

Introduction

Along with a warm heart and a generous spirit, for me, cooking is an essential element in turning a house into a home. But the essentials of home cooking are different for everyone. They change as we go through different stages of our lives—whether we're single, cooking with a partner or feeding a family. They also shift and adapt according to what is happening in the food world. Back in 1973, when I opened my cooking school, who would have thought that we would one day be eating calamari and sushi at all, let alone preparing it at home? People are traveling around the globe and bringing back taste memories that they want to have again and again. Markets sell the ingredients, and magazines, food shows and cookbooks offer the recipes. Home renovators are designing kitchens with restaurant-quality equipment, and every week a wonderful new gadget appears that makes cooking even easier. So why not cook?

I have witnessed many of these changes from the front lines, and visits to markets and restaurants around the world have influenced the way I cook, too. I have also learned a lot from the renowned teachers and chefs who have come to teach at my school over the years, from my association with the Heart and Stroke Foundation in producing three *HeartSmart*™ cookbooks, and from my students and customers, who always keep me on my toes with their questions and comments.

This book is a reflection of the way I am cooking now. It contains new recipes inspired by my recent travels and restaurant experiences, as well as some of my classic standbys and childhood favorites.

Along with the recipes, I have included thoughts about some aspects of food and cooking that are essential to me, such as seasonal foods, healthful cooking and cooking for children (as the mother of "selective" eaters, I have always been intensely interested in this subject, and it explains why I can never have too many chicken or pasta recipes, and why my fridge always contains iceberg lettuce!).

With the availability of so many restaurants, take-out options, catering and prepared foods, home cooking may seem almost unnecessary. Yet these days it is more important than ever. Though I am frequently away, my favorite place to be is home, and I think a lot of people feel the same way. So even frantically busy people are making the time to cook and eat dinners at home with their children and friends.

There are good reasons for this. Few things are more important than what we put in our bodies, and home cooking provides the best opportunity to choose the ingredients that go into our food. And we all want to spend more time with the people we care about. What better way than to linger over a meal with good conversation and good friends?

The essentials of home cooking may be different for everyone, but there is one thing that never changes, and that is using the freshest and best-quality ingredients and preparing them with care.

Bonnie Stern

Appetizers

In the world of food tasting and recipe testing, we do a lot of nibbling. At the cooking school we rarely eat a full serving of anything, so life tends to be one appetizer after another.

Many people love to eat this way, whether it means sampling canapes off a tray at a cocktail party, or ordering two appetizers at a restaurant instead of a main course.

Appetizers are especially popular when they are crispy on the outside and tender on the inside.

Restaurants achieve this easily by deep-frying, but I get there by using phyllo pastry, puff pastry, tortillas and crunchy coatings instead.

In this chapter I've also included a few of my favorite spreads and dips—serve one for a last-minute appetizer or place on the table as a substitute for butter.

Shrimp Ceviche

Ceviche is usually a dish of uncooked seafood that has been marinated in an acidic mixture of vinegar or lemon juice, which "cooks" the fish. This ceviche, however, is a bit of a misnomer, as it is made with cooked shrimp and is similar to a spicy citrus shrimp cocktail. Serve it on a bed of cilantro or in cocktail glasses as a first course.

2 lb (1 kg) extra-large shrimp
   (about 32 to 40), shelled and
   cleaned
1 cup (250 mL) lemon juice
1 tomato, seeded and diced
2 jalapeños, seeded and diced
1 small sweet onion, diced
1 tsp (5 mL) salt
1/4 cup (50 mL) chopped fresh
   cilantro

Sesame Chile Sauce
1/2 cup (125 mL) commercial chili
   sauce (e.g., Heinz), or ketchup
1 tbsp (15 mL) seasoned
   rice vinegar
1 tbsp (15 mL) sweet Thai chile
   sauce, or 1/2 tsp (2 mL) hot
   Asian chile paste
1/2 tsp (2 mL) roasted sesame oil

1. Bring a large pot of water to a boil. Add shrimp. Return to a boil and cook for 2 minutes, or just until shrimp curl and turn pink. Drain and place in a large bowl.

2. Meanwhile, in a small bowl, combine lemon juice, tomato, jalapeños, onion, salt and cilantro. Pour over shrimp. Marinate for 1 hour at room temperature or longer in refrigerator. Drain shrimp before serving.

3. For dipping sauce, in a small bowl, combine chili sauce, rice vinegar, sweet Thai sauce and sesame oil.

Makes 8 servings

Grilled Jumbo Shrimp

Shrimp are graded according to the number of shrimp per pound. When I really want to impress I use jumbo tiger shrimp, but this recipe also works well made with smaller shrimp (16 to 20 shrimp per pound—still pretty big). When the shrimp are large, you don't have to worry about them falling through the grill, but if you are cooking smaller ones, use a grilling basket or thread them on skewers.

Grill shrimp with or without the shells—they are less messy to eat if they have been peeled but have more flavor if the shells are left on. It is more economical to serve this as an appetizer (2 or 3 per person), but it also makes a wicked main course.

12 to 18 jumbo tiger shrimp
  (6 to 8 per lb/500 g), unpeeled
1/2 cup (125 mL) olive oil
2 tsp (10 mL) salt
1 tsp (5 mL) pepper
2 tbsp (25 mL) chopped fresh
  rosemary, or 1/2 tsp (2 mL) dried
4 cloves garlic, minced
1/2 tsp (2 mL) hot red pepper
  flakes

1. With scissors, cut shrimp shells along top to open. To clean, make a deep incision to remove the intestinal tract (sometimes called deveining). Flatten shrimp open but leave shells on.

2. In a small bowl, combine olive oil, salt, pepper, rosemary, garlic and hot pepper flakes.

3. Rub shrimp with olive oil mixture under shell and along incision. Marinate for up to 1 hour in refrigerator.

4. Grill shrimp for about 2 to 3 minutes per side, or just until flesh is white and opaque. Shells will be red. Do not overcook.

Makes 6 servings

Caramelized Onion and Gorgonzola Pizza

We used to call this a tart, but when Jacques Pépin had lunch with us at the cooking school while he was promoting his memoirs and said it was the best pizza he had ever eaten, we changed the name fast! Trust me, this one's a winner.

I often cook lots of onions and then freeze them in 3/4-cup (175 mL) amounts (enough for one pizza) so that I can whip this up quickly. Serve it in wedges with a salad for a first course or light lunch, or cut it into small squares for an appetizer.

2 tbsp (25 mL) olive oil

3 onions, chopped

1 tbsp (15 mL) brown sugar

2 tbsp (25 mL) balsamic vinegar

1/2 tsp (2 mL) salt

1/2 tsp (2 mL) pepper

8 oz (250 g) frozen puff pastry, or
  1/2 recipe homemade, cold

4 oz (125 g) Brie, rind removed,
  diced

4 oz (125 g) mild Gorgonzola or
  Cambozola, rind removed, diced

2 tbsp (25 mL) chopped fresh
  tarragon, or 1/4 tsp (1 mL) dried

1. Heat oil in a large deep skillet on medium-high heat. Add onions and cook for about 10 minutes, or until wilted and starting to brown. Add sugar, vinegar, salt and pepper. Reduce heat and cook gently, uncovered, for 15 to 25 minutes, or until richly caramelized. Cool. (You should have about 3/4 cup/175 mL.)

2. Roll pastry into a 10-inch (25 cm) square. Place pastry on a baking sheet lined with parchment paper. Prick with a fork in about 12 places.

3. Spread onions over pastry. Dot with cheese. Sprinkle with tarragon. Refrigerate if not baking immediately.

4. Bake in a preheated 400 F (200 C) oven for 18 to 20 minutes, or until cheese has melted and pastry is crisp. Cool for 5 minutes. Cut into wedges or squares.

Makes 6 to 8 servings

Nick Malgieri's Quick Puff Pastry

I never used to make puff pastry very often until pastry chef Nick Malgieri changed our lives with this quick version. We use it for the Caramelized Onion and Gorgonzola Pizza and the Homestyle Tarte Tatin (page 183). This recipe makes enough for two pizzas or two tarts.

Cut 1 1/4 cups (300 mL) cold butter into 1/2-inch (1 cm) cubes and refrigerate. Combine 1/2 cup (125 mL) cold water with 1 tsp (5 mL) salt and refrigerate. Place 2 cups (500 mL) all-purpose flour in food processor. Add 1/4 cup (50 mL) diced butter and pulse 12 times. Add remaining diced butter and pulse twice just to distribute into flour. Drizzle salted water over flour. Pulse 5 or 6 times. Turn mixture out and gather into a rough rectangle.

On a floured surface, roll dough into an 18- x 12-inch (45 x 30 cm) rectangle. Fold into thirds lengthwise. Roll up from short end and press into a rough square. Wrap well and refrigerate for a few days or freeze.

Makes about 1 1/2 lb (750 g)

Spinach and Feta Mini Strudels

This is an easy version of Greek spanakopita, as you form the pastry into rolls rather than fussy triangles. The little thin rolls are nice and crisp and you can cut them into bite-sized pieces. They freeze well cooked or uncooked. Bake them directly from the frozen state for 30 to 40 minutes, or reheat the frozen baked pastries for 20 to 25 minutes.

1 tbsp (15 mL) olive oil

1 small onion, finely chopped

2 cloves garlic, finely chopped

8 oz (250 g) feta cheese, crumbled

2 10-oz (300 g) packages frozen
   spinach, defrosted, squeezed
   dry and chopped
   (about 2 cups/500 mL)

2 eggs

3 tbsp (45 mL) chopped fresh dill

1/2 tsp (2 mL) pepper

Pinch grated nutmeg

12 oz (375 g) phyllo pastry
   (12 sheets)

1/2 cup (125 mL) dry
   breadcrumbs or panko

1/3 cup (75 mL) melted butter or
   olive oil, or a combination

2 tbsp (25 mL) water

1. Prepare filling by heating oil in a small skillet on medium-high heat. Add onion and garlic and cook for a few minutes until tender and fragrant. Transfer to a large bowl. Add cheese, spinach, eggs, dill, pepper and nutmeg and combine well.

2. Cover phyllo with plastic wrap and then a damp tea towel. Place breadcrumbs in a small dish. Combine melted butter and water in a separate dish and have a pastry brush at hand.

3. Arrange one sheet of pastry on work surface. Brush with butter mixture and sprinkle with breadcrumbs. Repeat with 2 more layers. Arrange 1 cup (250 mL) spinach/cheese mixture along one long edge of pastry. Roll up lengthwise, tucking in ends as you roll. Transfer to a baking sheet and score top of pastry (just through to filling) into 10 pieces (so it will be easier to slice later). Repeat until 4 rolls are made. Brush rolls with any extra butter.

4. Bake in a preheated 400 F (200 C) oven 20 to 25 minutes, or until well browned. Slice and serve warm or at room temperature.

Makes about 40 pieces

Chicken Quesadillas with Smoked Mozzarella

Although Mexican food has never really been that popular in Canada (yes, I know some people love it, but I am talking about the big picture), everyone loves quesadillas. There are so many variations made with different kinds of cheeses and salsas. Kids (even my kids) love them. Sometimes I make the quesadillas with just cheese inside and serve them with a sour cream or yogurt dip for kids and guacamole (page 21) for adults or more adventurous eaters.

1 1/2 cups (375 mL) shredded
   cooked chicken
   (about 4 oz/125 g)
2 cups (500 mL) grated smoked
   mozzarella cheese
1 tomato, seeded and diced
1 jalapeño, seeded and finely
   chopped
1 clove garlic, minced
1/2 cup (125 mL) chopped fresh
   cilantro
1 tsp (5 mL) salt
4 10-inch (25 cm) flour tortillas

1. In a large bowl, combine chicken, cheese, tomato, jalapeño, garlic, cilantro and salt.

2. Spread one-quarter of mixture over half of each tortilla. Fold unfilled side over and press gently.

3. Cook quesadillas on a barbecue or grill pan or in a large ungreased skillet for about 3 minutes per side, or until lightly browned and cheese has melted. Cool for 2 minutes. Cut each quesadilla into 4 wedges.

Makes 16 pieces

Old-fashioned Deviled Eggs

Deviled eggs have become popular again, and I am happy about that because I love them. They look very cute served in egg cups or on a large platter on a bed of alfalfa sprouts or watercress. Chop any leftovers for egg salad sandwiches.

12 eggs

1/4 cup (50 mL) mayonnaise

1 tbsp (15 mL) Dijon mustard

1 tsp (5 mL) salt

1 tbsp (15 mL) finely chopped
  fresh tarragon, or 1/4 tsp
  (1 mL) dried

1 tsp (5 mL) paprika
  (preferably smoked)

1. Bring a large saucepan of salted water to a boil (the salt will help seal any cracks if the eggs break). Gently place eggs in water and return to a boil. Turn off heat, cover tightly and let sit for 14 minutes.

2. Drain eggs and shake pan gently to crack shells. Add cold water and let sit to chill. Gently remove shells.

3. Cut eggs in half crosswise and gently scoop out yolks. Place whites, cut side up, on a tray (cut a tiny slice off pointed end if necessary to make eggs stand up).

4. In a bowl, mash yolks with mayonnaise, mustard, salt and tarragon. Pipe or spoon back into egg whites. Dust lightly with paprika.

Makes 24 halves

Grilled Vegetable Sushi Rolls with Wasabi Mayonnaise Some

people are afraid of sushi because they think it means raw fish. But sushi really just means vinegared rice. You can make the rolls with cooked fish or shellfish, vegetables, sweet omelettes, chicken teriyaki and even rare steak. For kids I use cucumber strips and sesame seeds and serve with soy sauce for dipping. Anything goes if you throw tradition to the wind.

2 cups (500 mL) uncooked
  Japanese short-grain rice
1/3 cup (75 mL) seasoned rice
  vinegar
8 spears asparagus, trimmed
8 shiitake mushrooms, stemmed
1 small red onion, sliced in
  thick rounds
1 medium zucchini
  (about 4 oz/125 g),
  cut lengthwise in 4 slices
1 tbsp (15 mL) roasted sesame oil
2 tbsp (25 mL) sesame seeds,
  divided
1 tbsp (15 mL) pepper
1 tbsp (15 mL) kosher salt
1 sweet red or yellow pepper
1/4 cup (50 mL) mayonnaise
2 tbsp (25 mL) prepared wasabi
4 sheets toasted nori
1/4 cup (50 mL) thinly sliced
  pickled ginger

1. Rinse rice in several changes of cold water (until water runs clear). Place in a saucepan with 2 1/2 cups (550 mL) cold water. Cover. Bring to a boil and boil for 1 minute. Reduce heat to low and cook for 10 minutes. Remove saucepan from heat and let rest for 15 minutes. At no time should you remove the lid. Fold in vinegar. Taste and add more vinegar if necessary (the taste will dissipate as the rice cools).

2. Brush asparagus, mushrooms, onion and zucchini with sesame oil and sprinkle with 1 tbsp (15 mL) sesame seeds, pepper and salt. Grill for a few minutes per side or until browned.

3. Grill pepper on all sides until blackened. Cool and peel. Remove core and seeds and cut pepper into strips.

4. Slice mushrooms and cut onion rounds in half.

5. In a small bowl, combine mayonnaise and wasabi.

6. To roll sushi, arrange a sheet of nori, bumpy side up, on a sudari (bamboo) mat or heavy-duty plastic bag. Dip your fingers in cold water and shake off excess. Gently pat scant 1 cup (250 mL) cooked rice over nori, leaving about 1/2 inch (1 cm) clear at one narrow end.

7. Wet fingers again and shake off excess water. Spread about 1 tsp (5 mL) wasabi mayonnaise across center of rice. Top with strips of grilled vegetables and ginger. Sprinkle with sesame seeds.

8. Using the mat, roll up nori, slightly dampening clear end with water to help seal. Repeat with remaining rolls. Serve immediately if possible but if not, wrap each roll in plastic wrap.

9. Using a sharp knife dipped in cold water, trim ends off rolls (a treat for the chef). Cut each roll in half and then cut each half into three or four slices. Wet knife slightly before each cut or wipe with a wet cloth.

Makes about 32 pieces

Wild Rice Pancakes with Maple Mayonnaise and Smoked Salmon

We made these pancakes topped with my favorite Wolfhead smoked salmon from New Brunswick when I taught a class to a group of students from California.

For brunch you can make 5-inch (12 cm) pancakes and serve them with the smoked salmon or even with bacon and eggs. Or you can add 2 tbsp (25 mL) granulated sugar, omit the pepper and serve them topped with maple syrup and blueberries.

Cook wild rice in a large pot of boiling salted water for 45 to 50 minutes, or until the grains pop open. Drain well. The rice will double or triple in volume.

3 eggs

1 cup (250 mL) buttermilk

2 tbsp (25 mL) vegetable oil

1 cup (250 mL) all-purpose flour

1 tsp (5 mL) baking soda

1/2 tsp (2 mL) salt

1/2 tsp (2 mL) pepper

1 cup (250 mL) cooked wild rice

1/2 cup (125 mL) mayonnaise, sour cream or yogurt cheese (page 23)

1 tbsp (15 mL) honey-style mustard

1 tbsp (15 mL) maple syrup

12 oz (375 g) smoked salmon, sliced

1. In a large bowl, beat together eggs, buttermilk and oil.

2. In a separate bowl, combine flour, baking soda, salt and pepper.

3. Whisk dry ingredients into large bowl. Stir in wild rice. (Batter should be the consistency of yogurt.)

4. Heat a large, lightly oiled nonstick skillet on medium-high heat. Add batter by the tablespoon to make 2-inch (5 cm) pancakes. Cook for 2 to 3 minutes on each side. Arrange in a single layer on a serving platter.

5. In a small bowl, combine mayonnaise, mustard and maple syrup.

6. Top each pancake with a spoonful of maple mayonnaise and a small slice of salmon.

Makes about 30 pancakes

Potato Crostini with Smoked Salmon

Potatoes can be used as a base for most crostini or bruschetta toppings, but this combination is especially good (you could also use thinly sliced rare roast beef or prosciutto instead of salmon). For brunch, arrange five or six potato slices overlapping in a circle and top with smoked salmon and horseradish cream. For a last-minute appetizer you could even use thick designer potato chips in place of the roasted potatoes. Serve in flat baskets on a bed of herbs.

4 baking potatoes or Yukon Gold
   potatoes (about 2 lb/1 kg total)
2 tbsp (25 mL) olive oil
1 tsp (5 mL) salt
1/2 tsp (2 mL) pepper
1 tbsp (15 mL) chopped fresh
   thyme, or 1/4 tsp (1 mL) dried
1 tbsp (15 mL) chopped fresh
   rosemary, or 1/4 tsp (1 mL) dried

Topping
3/4 cup (175 mL) sour cream or
   yogurt cheese (page 23)
1 tbsp (15 mL) grated white
   horseradish, approx.
1/2 tsp (2 mL) pepper
2 tbsp (25 mL) slivered fresh
   chives or arugula, divided
8 oz (250 g) smoked salmon,
   thinly sliced

1. Slice potatoes into rounds 1/2 inch (1 cm) thick.

2. In a large bowl, combine olive oil, salt, pepper, thyme and rosemary. Add potatoes and toss with olive oil mixture.

3. Arrange potatoes in a single layer on parchment-lined baking sheets. Roast in a preheated 400 F (200 C) oven for 40 to 45 minutes, or until cooked, browned and crispy. Turn potatoes halfway through cooking time.

4. For topping, in a small bowl, combine sour cream, horseradish, pepper and 1 tbsp (15 mL) chives. Taste and adjust seasonings if necessary.

5. Smear some topping on each potato. Fold a slice of smoked salmon on top and garnish with remaining 1 tbsp (15 mL) chives. Serve warm or at room temperature.

Makes about 32 pieces

Million-Dollar Satays with Charmoula Drizzle

If filet costs as much where you live as it does here, you'll know why we call these million-dollar satays. But these really do melt in your mouth and are perfect for a special dinner. You can also use leg of lamb, chicken or pork chops. Serve with the charmoula or peanut dip.

If I am making satays with chicken or boneless pork chops, I grill them whole and then cut them into strips and skewer them. That way the bamboo skewers do not burn up on the grill (even when you soak skewers they still tend to burn). Another trick is to place a strip of tinfoil along one edge of your grill and place the skewers on the foil to prevent burning.

We borrowed this delicious marinade from Hugh Carpenter, who teaches at my school every year. His flavorful and easy recipes always inspire us to cook.

2 lb (1 kg) beef filet

1/4 cup (50 mL) hoisin sauce

2 tbsp (25 mL) plum sauce

2 tbsp (25 mL) oyster sauce

Charmoula Drizzle

1 cup (250 mL) mayonnaise

3 cloves garlic, minced

1 tbsp (15 mL) lemon juice

1 tbsp (15 mL) Tabasco chipotle
sauce, or 1 tsp (5 mL) pureed
chipotles

1/2 tsp (2 mL) ground cumin

2 tbsp (25 mL) finely chopped
fresh cilantro

1. Cut filet in half crosswise. Slice each half into slices 1/4 inch (5 mm) thick. In a small bowl, combine hoisin sauce, plum sauce and oyster sauce and rub into steak.

2. Thread steak onto bamboo skewers that have been soaked in cold water. Grill for 1 minute per side.

3. For sauce, in a small bowl combine mayonnaise, garlic, lemon juice, chipotle sauce, cumin and cilantro.

4. Drizzle charmoula over steak or serve as a dipping sauce.

Makes about 30 pieces

Peanut Dip

In a food processor, blender or bowl, combine 3 tbsp (45 mL) peanut butter, 3 tbsp (45 mL) water, 2 tbsp (25 mL) honey, 2 tbsp (25 mL) soy sauce, 1/2 tsp (2 mL) roasted sesame oil and 1/4 tsp (1 mL) hot Asian chile paste.

Makes about 2/3 cup (150 mL)

Cumin

Madhur Jaffrey introduced me to the importance of roasting cumin, which brings out its nutty, rich flavor. Roast cumin seeds in a skillet on medium-high heat for 2 to 4 minutes, or until the seeds are reddish-brown and fragrant. Cool and grind in a spice grinder; store in a sealed bag in the freezer.

Teriyaki-glazed Mini Meatballs

Meatballs are making a big comeback on the cocktail party circuit. Comfort food while you are working a room can't be beat! These are also great for dinner served over rice. You can use ground beef, chicken, veal, pork, turkey or a combination. They are delicious served hot or at room temperature. Even kids love them.

A mini ice-cream scoop (slightly bigger than a melon baller) works well for shaping mini meatballs. It's also great for scooping cookie batter or making mini muffins and truffles.

When I serve these as an appetizer, I like to pile the meatballs in a pedestal bowl, with the skewers coming out at all angles.

1 lb (500 g) ground chicken, turkey, beef or pork

1 egg

3/4 cup (175 mL) fresh breadcrumbs or panko

2 tbsp (25 mL) soy sauce

2 tbsp (25 mL) rice wine

1 tbsp (15 mL) granulated sugar

2 tbsp (25 mL) finely chopped onion

2 tbsp (25 mL) finely grated carrot

1 tbsp (15 mL) vegetable oil

Orange Teriyaki Sauce

2 cups (500 mL) chicken stock

1/4 cup (50 mL) soy sauce

1/4 cup (50 mL) orange juice

1/2 cup (125 mL) rice wine

2 tbsp (25 mL) granulated sugar

1. In a large bowl, combine chicken, egg, breadcrumbs, soy sauce, rice wine, sugar, onion and carrot. Knead together lightly with your hands or a spoon. Shape mixture into 1-inch (2.5 cm) balls and place on a baking sheet lined with waxed paper or parchment paper.

2. In a large, deep nonstick skillet, heat oil on medium-high heat. Add meatballs and cook for 3 to 5 minutes, or until brown. Do this in two batches if necessary. Return all meatballs to skillet.

3. For sauce, add stock, soy sauce, orange juice, rice wine and sugar to skillet. Bring to a boil. Reduce heat and simmer gently, uncovered, for 10 to 15 minutes, or until meatballs are thoroughly cooked and juices are thick and slightly syrupy. Shake pan often during cooking.

Makes about 40 meatballs

Tuna Tapas

Tapas are called the "little dishes" of Spain. They can range from something very simple, like olives, to potato omelettes cut in bite-sized pieces. They began with the Spanish custom of bartenders placing little plates over glasses of sherry to keep out the flies. Soon complimentary savory bites were placed on the plates, and in fact, in many bars in Spain, tapas are still free.

In Spain, Italy and Portugal, light tuna packed in olive oil is used in pastas, salads and sandwiches. It has a lot more flavor than white tuna packed in water, so try it for a change.

Roast your own peppers or buy piquillos—small thin-skinned Spanish sweet peppers that come roasted in jars.

This filling also makes great tuna sandwiches.

1 can white tuna (approx.
   6 1/2 oz/160 g), drained
2 tbsp (25 mL) olive oil
1 tsp (5 mL) sherry vinegar
2 tbsp (25 mL) chopped hot
   pickled peppers
1/4 cup (50 mL) chopped black or
   green olives, or a combination
1 tbsp (15 mL) small capers
1/2 tsp (2 mL) salt
1/4 tsp (1 mL) pepper
12 thin slices crusty baguette,
   plain or grilled
24 thin strips roasted sweet red
   peppers (preferably piquillos)

1. Place tuna in a food processor with olive oil, vinegar, hot peppers, olives, capers, salt and pepper. Process until mixture holds together.
2. Spread a spoonful of tuna on each piece of bread.
3. Crisscross slices of red peppers on top of tuna.

Makes 12 appetizers

Mumbai Glazed Cashews with Black Pepper

During my first trip to India, I visited Ramanlal Vithaldas, the fantastic spice store in Mumbai (Bombay). The shop was filled with wonderful aromas and delicious treats. I brought home spicy black pepper cashews for everyone, and when they were gone I started making these. They are good for snacking but are also great sprinkled on salads or soups.

Be sure to use freshly ground black pepper in this recipe.

2 tbsp (25 mL) butter
1/4 cup (50 mL) corn syrup
2 tbsp (25 mL) water
1 1/2 tsp (7 mL) salt
2 tbsp (25 mL) pepper
1 lb (500 g) raw cashews

1. In a heavy saucepan, combine butter, corn syrup, water, salt and pepper. Bring to a boil.
2. Stir in cashews and coat well with butter mixture.
3. Spread nuts on a parchment-lined baking sheet. Bake in a preheated 250 F (120 C) oven for 1 hour, stirring every 15 minutes to separate nuts. Cool.

Makes about 4 cups (1 L)

Sugared Walnuts with Fleur de Sel

Fleur de sel is the much acclaimed (and expensive!) sea salt from Brittany, but is the secret ingredient to making these nuts so delicious. Serve them as a snack, an appetizer or as a garnish on salads or soups. I like to make lots and keep them in the freezer to have on hand.

2 cups (500 mL) walnut halves
1/3 cup (75 mL) granulated sugar
1 tsp (5 mL) fleur de sel or Maldon salt

1. Bring a large pot of water to a boil. Add walnuts and cook for 3 minutes. Drain and pat dry.
2. Combine walnuts with sugar in a heavy saucepan and cook on medium-high heat for 5 to 8 minutes, or until sugar melts, browns and coats nuts. Stir in salt.
3. Quickly spread nuts on a baking sheet lined with parchment paper. Bake in a preheated 350 F (180 C) oven for 10 minutes. Cool.

Makes about 2 cups (500 mL)

Thai Shrimp Dumplings with Orange Chile Dipping Sauce

Dumplings always seem complicated until you make your first batch. As soon as you realize how easy they are and how much people love them, you'll make them all the time. They can be frozen before cooking as long as the meat and/or fish has not been previously frozen. Or cook them and then freeze. Use shrimp, ground pork or chicken or a combination.

Be sure to use the sweet Thai chile sauce and not the really hot Asian chile paste. If you cannot find it, just use commercial chili sauce (e.g., Heinz) and add 1/2 tsp (2 mL) roasted sesame oil.

1 lb (500 g) cleaned shrimp

1 egg white

1 tbsp (15 mL) cornstarch

1 tbsp (15 mL) soy sauce

1 small jalapeño, chopped

1/2 cup (125 mL) chopped fresh
  cilantro

35 Chinese dumpling wrappers

1/2 cup (125 mL) pureed canned
  tomatoes

1/2 cup (125 mL) coconut milk

1 tbsp (15 mL) red Thai curry
  paste

1 tbsp (15 mL) granulated sugar

1 tbsp (15 mL) vegetable oil

Orange Chile Dipping Sauce

1/3 cup (75 mL) sweet Thai chile
  sauce or Sesame Chile Sauce
  (page 2)

1 tbsp (15 mL) undiluted orange
  juice concentrate

1. Place shrimp in a food processor and chop coarsely. Blend in egg white, cornstarch and soy sauce. Stir in jalapeño and cilantro.

2. Arrange dumpling wrappers on work surface (you may have to do this in batches) in a single layer. Place about 1 tsp (5 mL) filling in middle of each wrapper.

3. Place one dumpling in the palm of your hand. Bring up sides of wrapper to cover filling but leave top open. Squeeze lightly around the middle to give dumpling a "waist." Flatten dumpling gently. Arrange on a lightly oiled waxed-paper-lined baking sheet open side up. Continue until all filling is used. Refrigerate dumplings until ready to cook.

4. In a small bowl, combine tomatoes, coconut milk, curry paste and sugar.

5. Heat oil in a large nonstick skillet on medium-high heat. Arrange dumplings pinched side up in skillet. Cook for about 2 minutes, or until lightly browned on bottom.

6. Add tomato mixture to skillet. Cover pan and shake gently. Cook for about 5 minutes, or until filling feels firm.

7. For sauce, combine chile sauce with orange juice concentrate and serve with dumplings.

Makes about 35 dumplings

Grilled Garlic Bread

Everyone in my family loves this garlic bread. Use it as a base for spreads or serve it on its own. You can add 1 tbsp (15 mL) chopped fresh rosemary or thyme; pepper is a great addition, too.

I also like this made with rye bread, black bread and pita.

1/4 cup (50 mL) olive oil
3 cloves garlic, minced
1 tsp (5 mL) kosher salt
8 slices baguette (cut on the diagonal in pieces
  1/2 inch/1 cm thick)

1. In a small bowl, combine oil, garlic and salt.
2. Brush oil mixture on one side of each slice of bread.
3. Just before serving, grill bread for 1 to 2 minutes per side, or until browned with grill marks.

Makes 8 pieces

Smoked Whitefish Spread

I serve this subtle, smoky spread on potato crostini (page 12) or on wild rice pancakes (page 11), grilled pita or just plain bread or bagels.

8 oz (250 g) smoked whitefish, bones and skin
  removed (weight after boning)
2 tbsp (25 mL) chopped fresh chives or green onions
2 tbsp (25 mL) chopped fresh dill
1/4 cup (50 mL) mayonnaise
1 tbsp (15 mL) lemon juice, or to taste
Salt and pepper to taste
Sprigs fresh dill or chives for garnish

1. Finely chop fish (or puree lightly).
2. In a bowl, combine fish, chives, dill and mayonnaise. Taste and add lemon juice and salt and pepper if necessary. Garnish with dill.

Makes about 1 cup (250 mL)

Spicy Guacamole

Guacamole is a great dip for tortilla chips or soft flour or corn tortillas. It can also be used on burgers and grilled chicken sandwiches or in quesadillas (page 7), breakfast wraps (page 143) or burritos.

The small, wrinkled dark-green Haas avocados are sweeter and more buttery than the larger light-green ones. Always use ripe avocados. The unripe ones have little flavor but still have lots of calories! (Although avocados are high in fat, they contain one of the best fats—monounsaturated—and they are also rich in folate.)

1 plum tomato, seeded and diced
2 jalapeños, seeded and finely
  chopped
1/2 cup (125 mL) chopped
  fresh cilantro
1 clove garlic, minced
1 tsp (5 mL) salt
3 tbsp (45 mL) lime juice
2 avocados

1. In a large bowl, combine tomato, jalapeños, cilantro, garlic, salt and lime juice.

2. Just before serving, cut each avocado in half. Remove pit. Holding avocado half in your hand, carefully dice avocado by slicing down to skin. Gently scoop out diced flesh with a spoon. Add to tomato mixture and mash with a potato masher. Mixture can be as smooth or chunky as you wish. Taste and adjust seasonings if necessary. If not serving immediately, cover surface of guacamole directly with plastic wrap to prevent discoloring.

Makes about 1 1/2 cups (375 mL)

Hummos

Hummos is an essential item in everyone's recipe file. Even though it is made from "beans," everyone seems to love it—even teenaged girls. Serve it as a dip with vegetables or grilled pita as an appetizer, spread it on bread instead of mayonnaise in sandwiches, serve it in a vegetarian burger with grilled vegetables, or put it on the table instead of butter or olive oil.

There are many variations. Use a head of roasted garlic instead of the raw garlic, use half a roasted squash in place of half the chickpeas, substitute other beans like white cannellini beans, add other herbs, etc.

Canned chickpeas are among the best canned foods (along with canned plum tomatoes, tuna and salmon). You could cook your own chickpeas, but I find that unnecessary for hummos (though I do prefer home-cooked chickpeas in salads and soups). If you like your hummos very, very smooth, pass it through a food mill.

1 19-oz (540 mL) can chickpeas
(or 2 cups/500 mL cooked),
rinsed and drained
3 cloves garlic, minced
3 tbsp (45 mL) lemon juice
3 tbsp (45 mL) olive oil
1/3 cup (75 mL) tahini
(sesame seed paste), or more
to taste
1/2 tsp (2 mL) hot red pepper
sauce, or more to taste
1/2 tsp (2 mL) ground cumin
Salt and pepper to taste
2 tbsp (25 mL) chopped fresh
cilantro

1. In a food processor, puree chickpeas with garlic, lemon juice, olive oil, tahini, hot pepper sauce and cumin. Taste and adjust seasonings. Add salt and pepper if necessary.

2. Place in a serving bowl and sprinkle with cilantro.

Makes about 2 cups (500 mL)

Black Olive Spread

My friend Andrea Iceruk started cooking South American specialties when she married her Latin lover, Jorge. They love this dip and make it all the time. Be sure to use pressed cottage cheese, not the creamy kind that comes in containers. If you can't find spicy black olives, season the spread with salt, pepper and hot red pepper sauce to taste.

Use this as a spread on sliced baguette and top each piece with half a black olive for garnish.

1 cup (250 mL) pressed
  cottage cheese
1 cup (250 mL) pitted black olives
  (preferably spicy)
1/4 cup (50 mL) sour cream or
  yogurt cheese

1. In a food processor, combine cottage cheese, olives and sour cream. Process on/off until olives are chopped but not totally pureed.

Makes about 1 1/2 cups (375 mL)

Yogurt Cheese

Yogurt cheese is so versatile. You can use it in place of sour cream, cream cheese or whipped cream in many recipes. Be sure to use natural-style yogurt that does not contain any setting agents (I usually use 1 percent, but even fat free will work well). Yogurt cheese can be sweetened with sugar, honey or maple syrup and/or vanilla, liqueurs or grated orange peel and used on desserts. Or it can be used as a savory spread or dip with garlic and herbs, smoked salmon bits and dill, or diced veggies and black pepper.

To make yogurt cheese, line a strainer with cheesecloth or paper towel. Set it over a bowl. Place 3 cups (750 mL) unflavored yogurt in strainer. Cover with plastic wrap. Refrigerate for a few hours or overnight. (The longer it drains, the thicker it gets.) Discard drained liquid or use for cooking rice or baking bread. Place yogurt cheese in a bowl and refrigerate.

If you make yogurt cheese a lot (and I do), it is worth buying a yogurt strainer—a little box that comes with a special strainer inside and a lid. It holds 3 cups (750 mL) yogurt and is nice and compact in the refrigerator.

Makes 1 1/2 cups (375 mL)

Cheddar Thyme Gougère

Gougère is a savory, cheesy cream puff that is easy to make and very delicious. (The sweet version of this dough, pâte à choux, is used in eclairs and croquembouche.) Serve these on their own or fill with hummos (page 22) or a cheese spread.

1 cup (250 mL) water

1/3 cup (75 mL) butter, cut in bits

1 cup (250 mL) all-purpose flour

4 eggs

1 1/2 tsp (7 mL) salt

1 tsp (5 mL) pepper

1 1/2 cups (375 mL) grated
  Cheddar or Swiss cheese

1 tbsp (15 mL) chopped fresh
  thyme, or 1/2 tsp (2 mL) dried

1. Combine water and butter in a medium saucepan and bring to a boil. Remove from heat and stir in flour all at once. Keep stirring until dough comes away from sides of pan and forms a ball.

2. Return pan to medium heat and cook gently for 2 to 3 minutes, stirring constantly, until dough dries out a bit and leaves a thin film on bottom of pan. Transfer dough to a large bowl and let cool for 5 minutes.

3. With a wooden spoon or electric mixer, beat eggs into dough one at a time. Dough will slip and slide but keep mixing and it will come together. Beat in salt, pepper, cheese and thyme.

4. Drop dough by large spoonfuls on a parchment-lined baking sheet. Bake in a preheated 425 F (220 C) oven for 25 to 30 minutes, or until puffed and browned. Turn off oven, pierce each puff with tip of a knife and allow to cool in oven for 15 minutes. Serve warm or cold.

Makes about 30 puffs

Bonnie's Essentials: Drinks

I always like to welcome people into my home with a special drink—not necessarily alcoholic—that I have made just for that occasion. On a cold night it could be a warm apple cider with a cinnamon swizzle stick, or even a small shooter of hot soup served in an espresso cup.

But summer is the time for something fresh, fruity and refreshing. These are a few of my current favorites.

Caipirinha

This is a fabulous drink. It's exotic, fun and refreshing. Cachaça is a Brazilian brandy made from sugar cane, but you can also make this with vodka (call it a caipiroska). Play salsa music, but if you serve more than one, you may have to have a dance instructor standing by!

1/2 lime, cut in small pieces
2 tsp (10 mL) granulated sugar
3 tbsp (45 mL) cachaça or vodka
Small handful ice cubes

1. Place lime and sugar in an old-fashioned glass. Using a "muddler" or handle of a wooden spoon, smash lime with sugar. Pour into a cocktail shaker with cachaça and ice. Blend with about 20 good shakes and strain back into glass.

Makes 1 serving

Brazilian Sangria

When my good friend Mitchell Davis, director of publications for the James Beard Foundation, told me about a drink with wine and chopped limes, I took the idea a step further and created this version of sangria. It has the same effect as sangria, too—you don't think it is very strong, but the conversation seems to get louder as you drink it!

2 limes, cut in chunks
1/4 cup (50 mL) granulated sugar
1/4 cup (50 mL) cachaça or light rum
3 cups (750 mL) dry red wine (Rioja)
2 cups (500 mL) sparkling water, chilled
Ice

1. Place limes and sugar in bottom of a pitcher and crush with a wooden spoon.
2. Add cachaça and wine and refrigerate until ready to serve.
3. Add sparkling water and ice. Serve in big glasses.

Makes 8 servings

Cava Sangria

If we are lucky, when we have a special cooking class, Jeff Sansone, master mixologist at Toronto's Canoe Restaurant and Bar, creates special drinks for us. This sangria was developed for a Spanish entertaining class we held when I returned from Spain. Jeff had also just been to Spain and reported that sangria made with the famous Spanish sparkling white wine, cava, was all the rage (usually sangria is made with red wine).

For a non-alcoholic version, use ginger ale instead of cava, orange juice concentrate instead of the liqueurs and omit the brandy.

1/2 cup (125 mL) Spanish brandy

3/4 cup (175 mL) orange liqueur, lichee liqueur or
    melon liqueur, or a combination

4 cups (1 L) white cranberry juice

4 cups (1 L) tangerine juice or other pale fruit juice

1 cup (250 mL) fresh or frozen cranberries

2 oranges, thinly sliced

6 cups (1.5 L) cava or other sparkling white wine
    (2 bottles)

1. Combine brandy and liqueur in a large pitcher or
punch bowl.

2. Add cranberry juice, tangerine juice, cranberries and
orange slices. Refrigerate.

3. Add cava just before serving.

Makes about 12 servings

California Limeade

Homemade limeade or lemonade is a wonderful treat,
especially on hot days. The fizz of the sparkling water
makes it even more refreshing, and adding vodka gives
it a good kick. Make the full amount of sugar syrup
because it keeps for at least a month in the refrigerator
and is very good in mixed drinks, since the sugar is dissolved.

If you want to make this non-alcoholic, omit the vodka
and use less sugar syrup.

2 cups (500 mL) granulated sugar

2 cups (500 mL) water

1/4 cup (50 mL) fresh lime juice

1/4 cup (50 mL) vodka

Ice

1 cup (250 mL) sparkling water

1. Combine sugar and water in a saucepan and bring to
a boil. Reduce heat and cook gently for 2 to 3 minutes.
Cool.

2. Place 1/4 cup (50 mL) sugar syrup, lime juice and
vodka in a cocktail shaker with some ice. Shake until
very cold.

3. Place a few ice cubes in two tall glasses. Strain drink
into glasses. Add 1/2 cup (125 mL) sparkling water to
each glass.

Makes 2 big drinks

Sparkling Pomegranate Cooler

Pomegranate juice is delicious and full of antioxidants
(which are said to be very good for you), but it can be dif-
ficult to find. Look for it in Middle Eastern or Russian grocery stores. (You can also squeeze the juice from a fresh
pomegranate using a citrus press, or you can substitute
cranberry juice.)

1 tbsp (15 mL) orange liqueur

1 paper-thin orange slice

1/4 cup (50 mL) pomegranate juice

1/4 cup (50 mL) sparkling white wine

Pomegranate seeds, optional

1. Pour orange liqueur into a wine glass. Flatten orange
slice onto inside of glass (Orange slice must be paper
thin to stick.) Add juice and sparkling wine. Sprinkle with
a few pomegranate seeds.

Makes 1 serving

I'm a firm believer in the chef's saying that the job of a good cook is to use the best ingredients, and then don't mess them up. I can't stress how important it is to use the best-quality ingredients. That's what will make the biggest difference to your cooking.

One of the big advantages of home cooking is that you know exactly what is in your food, and you can make sure you are feeding your family and guests nothing but the best.

Here are ten ingredients that I use a lot, and that can truly make a difference to the outcome of a dish.

Ingredients

1. Cooking Oils

Although I love butter, with a few exceptions I save it for baking. In cooking I usually use **olive oil**. Not only is it healthful, but it adds a delicious flavor to foods. The best-quality oils have a fresh, fruity olive flavor and are not greasy or strong.

I buy the best extra-virgin oil for salads and a less expensive extra-virgin oil for cooking. Keep it in the cupboard and, once opened, use it within a few months.

When I do not want the taste of olive oil (e.g., in Asian recipes or most desserts), I use a mild-tasting vegetable oil like **sunflower** or **canola oil**. Vegetable oils do not keep indefinitely, either, so buy them in quantities that you will use up within a few months.

Dark roasted **sesame oil** is used in Asian dishes. It has a strong, nutty flavor and is used more as a seasoning than a cooking oil. A small amount will go a long way. Keep refrigerated once the bottle has been opened.

2. Vinegars

I use vinegars as a seasoning and in salad dressings (using a sweet, good-quality vinegar means you can use less oil). There are so many different kinds, but here are a few of my favorites.

Balsamic vinegar is traditionally made from the must of Trebbiano grapes. It is aged in casks of different woods descending in size as the vinegar evaporates. It is quite thick and syrupy and very sweet and viscous.

There are basically three types of balsamic vinegar. The original authentic type is made by families who have passed down their recipe from generation to generation. This vinegar is very expensive (about $200 Canadian for 4 oz/125 g) and is rarely used in salad dressings. It is drizzled sparingly over chunks of Parmigiano Reggiano for appetizers, over grilled veal or fish for main courses, and sometimes even over ice cream for dessert.

In cooking and salad dressings, I generally use the artisan balsamic, which is aged for less time and is available at more reasonable prices. And then there is the "overnight balsamic" that is sold at very low prices. It is generally not true balsamic at all but regular vinegar with flavor and color added.

I also use **red wine vinegar** and **white wine vinegar** in salad dressings and in cooking. It is hard to find good red and white wine vinegar, though I have recently found some really delicious wine vinegars from Spain that have been aged in casks of oak or chestnut. Although they are expensive, they are excellent, so watch out for them.

If I can't find a good red wine vinegar I often use **sherry vinegar**, which has a softer, more interesting flavor than most wine vinegars.

I generally do not use flavored vinegars. Instead I buy good-quality unseasoned vinegars and add herbs or flavorings to a dish as I need them.

Rice vinegar can be plain or seasoned. The seasoned version is made specifically for sushi and contains salt and sugar, but you can also use it in salad dressings. Because rice vinegar is very mild, you need very little oil. You can also use it instead of cider vinegar.

3. Salt

I generally use **kosher salt** in cooking. It is a very clean, mild coarse salt with small crystals, and I use it for everything. It does not contain iodine or anti-caking agents and is not as salty as regular table salt.

I also use specialty salts such as **fleur de sel** from Brittany and **Maldon salt** from England. It can be saltier than kosher salt, so be careful when using. I like to use it to season steaks, grilled fish and baked potatoes.

I rarely put salt on the table. Instead, I add it as I am cooking to bring out the flavor in foods (in the end, I think you use less salt). However, if you are cooking for people who are salt sensitive (e.g., hypertensive), let everyone season to taste at the table instead.

4. Pepper

Always use freshly ground pepper. Although peppercorns come in many colors and varieties, when it comes right down to it, all you need is basic black. I love the incredible Talamanka pepper from Honduras. Use a pepper grinder with an adjustable grind.

5. Fresh Herbs

Use fresh herbs quickly and use lots. They will add the taste of summer and sunshine to your food.

I like to have a selection of fresh herbs on hand. I usually keep fresh chives or green onions, dill, parsley, cilantro, rosemary, tarragon and thyme in the refrigerator. Wash fresh herbs and dry them well. Wrap in paper towels or tea towels and store in a sealed container or plastic bag. Some herbs keep better than others. Parsley, for example, keeps for a couple of weeks, but basil only keeps for a couple of days.

Although some cookbooks recommend substituting one-third the amount of dried herbs for fresh, my rule is to be very generous with fresh herbs and very stingy with dried.

6. Garlic

Always use fresh garlic. Garlic powder and the chopped garlic sold in jars are poor substitutes for the real thing. If you smell the bottled or powdered garlic next to fresh you will know they are not the same. Peel garlic by gently smashing the cloves with the flat side of a knife or a meat pounder. The peels should slip right off.

If a recipe calls for powdered garlic (e.g., in a rub), use the granulated variety, and make sure it is very fresh; otherwise it can add a bitter taste to food.

7. Fresh Lemons and Limes

There is nothing like fresh lemon and lime juice. The bottled stuff doesn't come close. To juice lemons and limes easily, pierce the fruit, place in a small bowl and heat for about 30 seconds in the microwave; the juice will pour out (I am exaggerating a bit). Grate lemons and limes before heating and freeze the peel if you are not using it. You can also freeze the juice in ice-cube trays.

8. Hot Seasonings

Jalapeños, banana peppers, serranos and habañeros are all fresh hot peppers that are fairly easy to find. Jalapeños are the mildest; habañeros are very hot. Most of the recipes in this book that call for hot fresh peppers specify jalapeños, but you can substitute hotter peppers if you like. For a milder flavor, remove the ribs and seeds. (If you accidentally add too many hot peppers, try a tip I learned from Zal Yanovsky and add a little lime juice to cut the heat.)

Chipotles are smoked jalapeños that usually come packed in adobo, a spicy tomato sauce. They have become so popular that there is even a Tabasco chipotle sauce. I use chipotles a lot, because they add a unique smoky flavor to food as well as heat. You can substitute chopped jalapeños, but they will not give you the same smoky taste. I usually use canned chipotles. When I buy a can, I puree the peppers in the adobo sauce and freeze the puree flat in a small, heavy-duty resealable plastic bag. That way I can break off a little piece when I need some. (This is also a great way to freeze coconut milk, tomato paste, etc.)

Chipotle powder (dried and ground chipotles) is also available, and I use it in rubs (1/2 tsp/2 mL powder = 1 tsp/5 mL pureed chipotles).

I also use a lot of Spanish smoked paprika. It can be hot or sweet, and it has a delicious smoky flavor.

As a basic all-purpose hot red pepper sauce, I love Tabasco. It has been made the same way, with the same three ingredients (chiles, salt and water) for more than 125 years. Although there are many other hot sauces, I always know just how hot Tabasco will be.

I use two types of Asian chile seasonings and they are very different. **Hot Asian chile paste** is a combination of chiles, vinegar, garlic and salt. Use it sparingly, as it is very hot. **Thai sweet chile sauce** is a hot-sweet blend of red chiles, sugar, garlic, vinegar and salt. It is quite mild and can be used on its own as a dipping sauce for spring rolls, satays or dumplings.

There are several kinds of **curry seasonings**. Indian curry powders and pastes are combinations of spices (up to thirty different kinds), such as chiles and coriander. I use the Patak brand, which is readily available. Thai curry pastes are blends of herbs, citrus and onion. They can be red or green. I prefer curry paste over curry powder because it does not have a dry, raw flavor.

9. Chocolate

Always use the best-quality chocolate. One of my favorite brands is Callebaut, a Belgian chocolate that comes in blocks and calets (chips). Though other chocolates are smoother for eating, Callebaut is great for baking, and it has a rich chocolate flavor and is usually easy to find.

To melt chocolate, chop it into small pieces and melt it slowly over low, indirect heat (e.g., in a double boiler over barely simmering water). If you use a microwave, use Medium (50%) heat and check every thirty seconds. Remove the chocolate from the heat before it has completely melted and stir until smooth (remember that chocolate melts in your hand, so it doesn't require much heat).

I use four different kinds of chocolate—unsweetened, milk, dark and white. **Unsweetened chocolate** has the most chocolate flavor, but it contains no sugar and is only used in baking (don't even consider snacking on it). It will keep in a cool place for at least two years.

Dark chocolate can be either **bittersweet** or **semisweet**. Bittersweet has more chocolate and less sugar, but the two can be used interchangeably. It will keep in a cool cupboard for about one year.

Milk chocolate is my favorite eating chocolate (obviously I am not a chocoholic). Because it does not have as strong a chocolate taste as dark chocolate, it is not used often in baking, but I do like to use milk chocolate chips in cookies and muffins. It will keep in a cool cupboard for a couple of months.

White chocolate is extremely variable. Good-quality white chocolate takes less time to melt than dark chocolate, but some brands do not melt as well as others. Buy a brand that contains cocoa butter, not vegetable fat. It will keep in a cool place for a couple of months.

Cocoa powder is unsweetened chocolate with almost all the cocoa butter removed. I like to use imported Dutch-processed cocoa, which is less acidic and darker in color than regular cocoa. Be sure to sift it just before using.

10. Vanilla

Vanilla is the aroma of home baking. Use only pure vanilla. Nielsen-Massey vanilla is one of my favorites and it now also comes as a paste based on glucose rather than alcohol. The vanilla seeds are still in it, and they look wonderful in meringues, custards or cheesecakes. There is also a new vanilla powder, made without sugar or alcohol, which can be used when you don't want additional liquid or color (use the same quantity of vanilla paste or powder as you would vanilla extract).

If you store whole vanilla beans in your sugar cannister, the sugar will take on a wonderful vanilla taste and fragrance.

Soups

I went to Europe for the first time when I was in university. I traveled with my best friend, Andrea Iceruk. We covered about twelve countries in three months. When we got to Stockholm, a friendly sales clerk in a department store invited us home for dinner.

We were getting pretty homesick by this time, so we were especially grateful. She made us a heartwarming cream of celery soup, and to this day it tastes comforting, friendly and homey to me.

I think soup should be like that—soul-satisfying, reassuring and warm.

Chicken Soup with Kreplach

For me, chicken soup is the heart of both family life and good cooking. It is great on its own or served with noodles, matzo balls or kreplach. It can also be diluted and used in other soups or in rice pilaf. It even cures a cold!

Use the best-quality chicken you can find—kosher, organic or free-range.

1 4-lb (2 kg) chicken

2 onions, peeled and quartered

2 stalks celery with leaves, sliced

2 carrots, sliced

2 parsnips, peeled and sliced

1 bunch fresh parsley

1 bay leaf

1 tsp (5 mL) salt

1/4 tsp (1 mL) pepper

30 kreplach

1. Cut chicken into about 10 pieces. Remove and discard any visible fat. Place in a large pot (a pasta pot with strainer works well) and add cold water just to cover chicken. Bring to a boil and skim off scum that rises to surface.

2. Add onions, celery, carrots, parsnips, parsley, bay leaf, salt and pepper. Bring to a boil again, reduce heat and simmer very gently, covered, for 2 hours.

3. Strain soup into another pot. Taste and add salt and pepper if necessary. Use chicken to make kreplach, or use in soup or sandwiches. Skim fat off surface of soup with a big spoon, or refrigerate soup overnight and then discard solidified fat on surface.

4. When ready to serve, add kreplach to hot soup and simmer gently for 5 minutes to heat. Taste and adjust seasonings if necessary.

Makes 8 to 10 servings

Matzo Balls

In a bowl, beat 1 egg with 2 egg whites. Add 1/2 cup (125 mL) matzo meal, 1 1/2 tsp (7 mL) salt, 2 tbsp (25 mL) chicken stock and 2 tbsp (25 mL) chopped fresh parsley. Cover and refrigerate for 30 minutes.

With wet hands, shape mixture into 10 to 12 balls.

Gently add matzo balls to a large pot of boiling water and simmer, covered, for 40 minutes. Remove from water and serve in chicken soup.

Makes 10 to 12 balls

Kreplach

Kreplach are dumplings made with a pasta-like dough and stuffed with meat, poultry or vegetables. They are served in chicken soup instead of matzo balls, though it is hard to decide which is better. You can also fry them after the initial cooking and serve with browned onions.

Kreplach are usually more of a production to make than matzo balls because of the dough, but this version will change all that. Kreplach and matzo balls are cooked separately in boiling water so as not to cloud the soup. This is fusion cooking at its best—traditional Jewish dumplings made easy with the use of Chinese dumpling wrappers.

1 tbsp (15 mL) vegetable oil

1 small onion, chopped

4 oz (125 g) shiitake mushrooms, stemmed and chopped (about 2 cups/500 mL)

1 cup (250 mL) diced cooked chicken

1 tsp (5 mL) salt

2 tbsp (25 mL) chopped fresh parsley

1 egg

30 Chinese dumpling wrappers

1. Heat oil in a medium skillet on medium-high heat. Add onion and cook until browned, about 5 minutes. Add mushrooms and cook for about 5 minutes, or until liquid has evaporated. Remove from heat and stir in chicken, salt and parsley.

2. Chop mixture in a food processor or by hand. Mix in egg.

3. Arrange wrappers on counter and place a round teaspoon of filling on each. Do not overfill. Moisten edges of wrappers with water and fold sides over filling. Pinch edges together to seal.

4. Bring a large pot of water to a boil. Add kreplach and cook for 10 minutes. Drain and add to soup. (To make ahead and freeze, place cooked dumplings on baking sheets lined with lightly oiled waxed paper. When frozen, transfer to freezer bags.)

Makes 30 dumplings

Wild Mushroom Soup with Mushroom Sauté

Fresh wild mushrooms are expensive, but, boy, can they make a soup taste good. Save the most exotic mushrooms for the garnish, and if you can't find them, just use creminis or portobellos, or even plain button mushrooms.

As an extra garnish for this soup, drizzle a little thinned sour cream around the edge of each serving.

1/2 oz (15 g) dried wild
   mushrooms
1 cup (250 mL) warm water
1 tbsp (15 mL) olive oil
2 shallots, chopped
1 1/2 lb (750 g) fresh cremini
   and/or portobello mushrooms,
   trimmed and sliced (about
   12 cups/3 L)
1 potato, peeled and diced
4 cups (1 L) chicken stock or
   vegetable stock
1 tsp (5 mL) salt
1/4 tsp (1 mL) pepper
2 tbsp (25 mL) lemon juice
1 tsp (5 mL) white truffle oil,
   optional

Garnish

1 tbsp (15 mL) olive oil
2 cloves garlic, finely chopped
1 lb (500 g) assorted fresh wild
   mushrooms (e.g., oyster, shiitake,
   chanterelles, etc.), stemmed and
   sliced
1/4 tsp (1 mL) salt
1/4 tsp (1 mL) pepper
1 tbsp (15 mL) chopped fresh
   tarragon

1. Place dried mushrooms in a small bowl. Cover with warm water and let soften for 30 minutes. Strain liquid through cheesecloth or paper towel-lined strainer and reserve liquid. Rinse mushrooms well and chop.

2. Heat olive oil in a large saucepan on medium-high heat and add shallots. Cook for a few minutes until tender.

3. Add cremini mushrooms and chopped soaked mushrooms to saucepan. Add potato, stock, mushroom-soaking liquid, salt and pepper. Bring to a boil. Reduce heat and simmer gently for 15 to 20 minutes, or until potato is tender.

4. Puree soup. Taste and adjust seasonings if necessary. Add lemon juice and truffle oil if using. Add more stock if soup is too thick.

5. Meanwhile, for garnish, heat olive oil in a large skillet on medium-high heat. Add garlic and cook for 1 to 2 minutes, or until tender. Add sliced wild mushrooms. Cook for 5 to 10 minutes, or until any liquid evaporates. Season with salt, pepper and tarragon.

6. If using sour cream garnish, in a small measuring cup, combine sour cream with 1 tbsp (15 mL) milk. Add milk until mixture is consistency of whipping cream.

7. Place a spoonful of sautéed mushrooms on each serving of soup.

Makes 8 servings

Cremini Mushrooms

Creminis are brown button mushrooms with a great name. When left to grow bigger, they turn into portobellos. If a recipe calls for portobello mushrooms and they are going to be chopped, use creminis instead, as they are less expensive than portobellos.

Tortilla and Chicken Soup

I was so excited the first time I had tortilla soup. It was comforting and familiar and yet exotic at the same time.

You can place the garnishes in the individual bowls before adding the soup, sprinkle the garnishes on the soup just before serving, or let guests add their own. Everything can be prepared ahead except for the avocado, which should be diced at the last minute so that it does not discolor.

1 tbsp (15 mL) olive oil

1 onion, chopped

2 cloves garlic, finely chopped

1 jalapeño, seeded and chopped

1 tsp (5 mL) ground cumin

6 cups (1.5 L) chicken stock

1 tsp (5 mL) salt

2 cups (500 mL) shredded
   cooked chicken

2 cups (500 mL) fresh or frozen
   corn kernels (2 ears)

2 tbsp (25 mL) lime juice

Garnish

2 cups (500 mL) crushed
   tortilla chips

1/4 cup (50 mL) chopped
   fresh cilantro

2 tomatoes, seeded and diced

2 cups (500 mL) grated Monterey
   Jack or smoked mozzarella
   cheese

1 avocado, diced

1. Heat oil in a large saucepan or Dutch oven on medium heat. Add onion and garlic and cook for 3 to 4 minutes, or until translucent. Stir in jalapeño and cumin and cook for 1 to 2 minutes, or until very fragrant.

2. Add chicken stock and salt. Bring to a boil. Add chicken and corn. Reduce heat and simmer, covered, for 5 minutes.

3. Add lime juice. Remove from heat. Taste and adjust seasonings if necessary.

4. Serve soup in bowls and garnish with tortilla chips, cilantro, tomatoes, cheese and avocado.

Makes 6 to 8 servings

San Marzano Tomato Soup

San Marzano tomatoes are grown in the volcanic soil near Naples and are reputed to be the best in the world. I have used them for years in my tomato sauces but never thought they would make such a difference in tomato soup. For a spicier soup, add hot red pepper sauce or hot Asian chile paste to taste at the end.

As a garnish for this soup, I drizzle a little thinned sour cream around the edge of each bowl and then place a spoonful of Honey Tomato Jam in the center.

1 tbsp (15 mL) olive oil

1 onion, chopped

2 cloves garlic, finely chopped

1/4 tsp (1 mL) hot red
   pepper flakes

1 carrot, chopped

1 stalk celery, chopped

1 28-oz (796 mL) can
   San Marzano plum tomatoes,
   with juices

2 cups (500 mL) chicken stock,
   vegetable stock or water

1 tsp (5 mL) salt

1/4 tsp (1 mL) pepper

1. Heat oil in a large saucepan on medium heat. Add onion, garlic and hot pepper flakes and cook gently for 3 to 5 minutes, or until softened. Add carrot and celery. Cook very gently for 5 minutes.

2. Add tomatoes and juices, breaking up tomatoes with a wooden spoon. Add stock and bring to a boil. Reduce heat and simmer, covered, for 20 minutes. Add salt and pepper.

3. Puree soup and return to heat. Taste and adjust seasonings if necessary.

Makes 6 to 8 servings

Honey Tomato Jam

Spread this on bread for an appetizer or serve on the table instead of butter. The jam can also be used as a sauce on grilled chicken or lamb chops.

Heat 1 tbsp (15 mL) olive oil in a large skillet on medium heat. Add 1 chopped onion, 3 finely chopped garlic cloves and 1 tbsp (15 mL) chopped fresh ginger and cook gently for 3 to 5 minutes, or until tender. Add 1/2 tsp (2 mL) ground cinnamon, 1/2 tsp (2 mL) ground cumin and a pinch hot red pepper flakes and cook for 1 minute.

Add one 28-oz (796 mL) can chopped plum tomatoes and their juices and bring to a boil. Reduce heat to low and simmer, uncovered, for 20 to 25 minutes, or until thick.

Add 3 tbsp (45 mL) honey, 2 tbsp (25 mL) lemon juice and 1/2 tsp (2 mL) salt. Cook for another few minutes. Taste and adjust seasonings if necessary.

Makes about 2 cups (500 mL)

Thai Carrot and Ginger Soup

Many food critics are saying that the fusion-food trend is over, but I say it has just become part of the way we cook. Here's a good example. In this recipe, Thai flavors are incorporated into a traditional carrot soup.

1 tbsp (15 mL) olive oil

1 onion, chopped

2 cloves garlic, chopped

1 tbsp (15 mL) chopped
  fresh ginger

2 tsp (10 mL) red Thai curry paste

2 lb (1 kg) carrots (about 6 large),
  grated or very thinly sliced

4 cups (1 L) chicken stock,
  vegetable stock or water

1 tbsp (15 mL) honey

1 tbsp (15 mL) lemon juice

1 tsp (5 mL) salt

1/4 tsp (1 mL) pepper

3/4 cup (175 mL) coconut milk

2 tbsp (25 mL) chopped
  fresh cilantro

1/4 cup (50 mL) shredded
  coconut, toasted

1. Heat oil in a large saucepan or Dutch oven on medium heat. Add onion, garlic and ginger. Cook gently until very fragrant, about 5 minutes. Add curry paste and cook for 30 seconds.

2. Add carrots, stock, honey, lemon juice, salt and pepper. Bring to a boil, reduce heat and simmer, covered, until carrots are tender, about 15 to 20 minutes.

3. Puree soup with an immersion blender or in a food processor or blender. Return to heat. Add coconut milk and heat for 5 minutes. Taste and adjust seasonings if necessary.

4. In a small bowl, combine cilantro and coconut. Sprinkle a bit of mixture on each serving.

Makes 6 to 8 servings

Coconut Milk
I like the coconut milk that comes in cans from Thailand or in Tetra Paks from the Philippines. It is a creamy alternative to dairy products and is used extensively in Asian cooking. Stir it well, and if it is thick, add water. Once opened, it deteriorates quickly, so freeze what you do not use. Freeze flat in resealable heavy-duty plastic bags and then break off what you need.
  You can also buy light coconut milk.

Red Lentil Soup

Lentil soup used to be considered an exotic Middle Eastern specialty, but it has become a family staple. It is comforting, hearty, vegetarian, healthful and delicious all at the same time. It freezes well, but if you make it ahead you will probably have to thin it when reheating.

1 cup (250 mL) dried red lentils

1 tbsp (15 mL) vegetable oil

3 cloves garlic, finely chopped

1 large onion, chopped

1 tsp (5 mL) ground cumin

2 tbsp (25 mL) grated carrot

6 cups (1.5 L) water

2 tsp (10 mL) salt

1/4 tsp (1 mL) pepper

1 tbsp (15 mL) lemon juice

2 tbsp (25 mL) chopped fresh coriander

1 lemon, cut in wedges

1. Place lentils in a sieve and rinse a few times. Spread out on a baking sheet. Pick them over and discard any stones.

2. Heat oil in a large saucepan or Dutch oven on medium heat. Add garlic and onion and cook gently for 3 to 4 minutes, or until tender and fragrant. Add cumin and carrot and cook until fragrant, about 30 seconds.

3. Add lentils and water. Bring to a boil. Reduce heat and simmer gently, covered, for 30 to 45 minutes, or until lentils are very tender and mixture is thick. Add salt and pepper.

4. If soup is too thick, add stock or water. Add lemon juice. Taste and adjust seasonings if necessary. Serve garnished with coriander and lemon wedges.

Makes 6 to 8 servings

Chunky Potato Soup with Dill

This soup is so simple but so delicious, and you probably have most of the ingredients on hand. Cut the vegetables into small or large chunks, as you wish.

1 tbsp (15 mL) vegetable oil

1 onion, chopped

1 clove garlic, finely chopped

2 carrots, sliced

2 stalks celery, sliced

4 large Yukon Gold potatoes, peeled and cut in chunks
  (about 2 lb/1 kg total)

6 cups (1.5 L) chicken stock, vegetable stock or water

1 tsp (5 mL) salt

1/4 tsp (1 mL) pepper

2 tbsp (25 mL) chopped fresh dill

1. Heat oil in a large pot on medium-high heat. Add onion and garlic and cook until tender and translucent, about 5 minutes.

2. Add carrots and celery and cook for 2 minutes. Add potatoes and stock and bring to a boil. Reduce heat and simmer, covered, until potatoes are very tender, about 20 minutes.

3. Puree half the soup with an immersion blender or in a food processor or blender (leave rest of soup chunky). Thin soup if necessary with additional stock or water. Add salt, pepper and dill. Cook for a few minutes longer. Taste and adjust seasonings if necessary.

Makes 6 to 8 servings

Celery Soup with Walnuts and Blue Cheese

Celery is sometimes overlooked, and it's a shame because it has so much flavor. Although there isn't any milk or cream in this soup, it tastes very rich and creamy. Serve it with garlic pita wedges (page 20) or crackers.

Some people think blue cheese is too strong, but mild versions such as Cambozola, mild Gorgonzola or Bleu de Bresse are creamy, rich and truly irresistible. However, you could also use Brie or Camembert in this recipe.

1 tbsp (15 mL) olive oil or butter

1 onion, chopped

5 stalks celery, sliced
  (about 1 lb/500 g total)

3 potatoes, peeled and chopped
  (about 1 lb/500 g total)

4 cups (1 L) chicken stock,
  vegetable stock or water

1 tsp (5 mL) chopped fresh thyme,
  or pinch dried

1 tsp (5 mL) salt

1/2 tsp (2 mL) pepper

1/2 cup (125 mL) chopped
  toasted walnuts

1/2 cup (125 mL) crumbled mild
  blue cheese, rind removed

1. Heat oil in a large saucepan or Dutch oven on medium heat. Add onion and cook for a few minutes until tender.

2. Add celery and cook for 5 minutes. Add potatoes, stock, thyme, salt and pepper. Bring to a boil. Reduce heat and cook gently, covered, for 30 minutes.

3. Puree soup. Strain if you wish. If soup is too thick, add a little more stock or water. Taste and adjust seasonings if necessary.

4. Sprinkle each serving with walnuts and cheese.

Makes 6 servings

Seasonal Foods

When we had a cottage in northern Ontario, we would always stop at a farmer's stand for fresh corn on our way home in late August. My husband, Ray, would swing into the line of cars on the roadside while I jumped out and bought the corn. It was our standard rou-tine, and we thought we had it down pat until the time I hurried back into the car with the corn and waited for Ray to drive back onto the highway. When the car didn't budge I looked over—to find that Ray had pulled ahead in the line, and I was sitting in someone else's car staring at a complete stranger. My husband was not amused ("Trying out another family, honey?").

But freshly picked produce is worth going through a bit of humiliation for, especially when the growing season is so short. Although we would like to, it is impractical for us to eat only local, seasonal produce year round. And as a cook it is hard to ignore the wonderful foods that come from countries around the world. But I do support our farmers by buying local produce whenever possible, and you should, too. It is also good for everyone—from children to professional chefs—to know where our food comes from and what goes into producing it. Many people are tending their own vegetable gardens; others are making pick-your-own trips to a local apple orchard or berry farm an annual family outing.

When things like fresh asparagus, strawberries, corn or wild blueberries are in season, it is a big reason to celebrate. If the journey from the field to the plate is quick, and your ingredients are very fresh, food needs very little embellishment.

Local Asparagus Soup
This soup really tastes exactly like asparagus, and we often make it in our classes.

2 lb (1 kg) asparagus, trimmed

1 tbsp (15 mL) olive oil

1 onion, chopped

3 cups (750 mL) chicken stock
   or vegetable stock

1 tsp (5 mL) salt

1/4 tsp (1 mL) pepper

2 tbsp (25 mL) chopped
   fresh chives

1. Cook asparagus in a deep skillet of boiling water for about 2 minutes. Chill under cold running water to set color. Drain well. If you wish, cut off about 12 tips and reserve for garnish. Dice remaining asparagus.

2. Heat oil in a saucepan on medium heat. Add onion. Cook gently for a few minutes until tender and fragrant. Add stock. Bring to a boil, reduce heat and simmer gently, covered, for 5 minutes.

3. Add asparagus and cook for 3 to 5 minutes longer, or until asparagus is tender (do not overcook, or soup will lose its vibrant color). Add salt and pepper and puree until smooth.

4. Taste and adjust seasonings. Serve soup garnished with fresh chives.

Makes 6 servings

Asparagus

Buy asparagus with tightly closed tips, and rinse it well. If your asparagus is very sandy, soak it in a bowl of warm water until the grit settles to the bottom of the bowl. Repeat until the asparagus is clean.

Try to buy stalks that are about the same thickness so they will cook evenly. (I prefer fat, juicy stalks.) Trim about 1 inch (2.5 cm) off the bottoms and then peel a couple of inches up the stalks using a vegetable peeler.

I cook asparagus lying flat in a skillet; the tips and peeled stalks take about the same amount of time to cook.

Split Pea Soup with Dill

This is perfect comfort food for a cold winter day, and it's one of my all-time favorites. It's good for you, too—low in fat and full of healthful legumes. It can also be served as a vegetarian main course.

If you make the soup ahead, you'll probably have to thin it with extra water when reheating. Be sure to check it for seasoning, too.

1 tbsp (15 mL) vegetable oil

1 onion, chopped

2 cloves garlic, finely chopped

1 large parsnip, peeled and diced

1 carrot, peeled and diced

1 cup (250 mL) dried split
  green peas, rinsed

10 cups (2.5 L) water

2 tsp (10 mL) salt

1/4 tsp (1 mL) pepper

1 cup (250 mL) broken
  dried spaghetti

2 tbsp (25 mL) chopped fresh dill

1. Heat oil in a large saucepan on medium heat. Add onion and garlic and cook until fragrant and tender, about 3 to 4 minutes.

2. Add parsnip and carrot and cook for 5 minutes. Add peas and combine well.

3. Add water and bring to a boil. Reduce heat and cook gently, covered, for 40 to 45 minutes, or until peas are very tender. Add salt and pepper. If you wish, puree all or part of soup.

4. Add spaghetti. Cook for 10 minutes, or until tender. Add water if soup is too thick. Taste and adjust seasonings if necessary. Sprinkle with dill.

Makes 8 to 10 servings

Pot au Feu

Pot au feu is one of my favorite French bistro dishes. But be warned, it is very simple.

I like this best served all together as a main course, but you can also have it the traditional way—serving the broth first and the meat and vegetables as the main course. I cook the potatoes separately so that the broth does not become cloudy, and you can serve it with the mustard mayo or roasted garlic mayonnaise (page 116). If you have fleur de sel, the outrageously expensive French sea salt, this is the time to use it. Sprinkle it on the soup when serving or mound a little on the plate as a condiment for dipping.

2 lb (1 kg) beef short ribs,
   cut in chunks

2 lb (1 kg) beef brisket,
   in one piece

16 cups (4 L) cold water

1/4 cup (50 mL) fresh
   parsley sprigs (with stems)

1 tbsp (15 mL) fresh thyme sprigs,
   or 1/2 tsp (2 mL) dried

1 bay leaf

1 3-lb (1.5 kg) chicken,
   cut in pieces

3 carrots, peeled and sliced on
   the diagonal

3 stalks celery, sliced on
   the diagonal

3 onions, peeled and cut in
   quarters

3 parsnips, peeled and sliced on
   the diagonal, optional

2 tsp (10 mL) salt

1/4 tsp (1 mL) pepper

2 lb (1 kg) baby potatoes

1 tbsp (15 mL) Dijon mustard

1/4 cup (50 mL) mayonnaise

1. Place short ribs and brisket in a large Dutch oven and cover with water. Bring to a boil. Discard scum as it rises. Reduce heat and simmer gently, covered, for 1 1/2 hours.

2. With string, tie parsley, thyme and bay leaf in a little bundle and add to soup.

3. Remove skin and visible fat from chicken. Add chicken to pot with beef. Bring to a boil again. Reduce heat and simmer gently, covered, for 30 minutes. Add water if necessary to keep ingredients covered.

4. Add carrots, celery, onions, parsnips if using, salt and pepper. Simmer gently, covered, for 30 to 45 minutes, or until beef is very tender, chicken is cooked and vegetables are very tender but not falling apart. Taste and adjust seasonings if necessary.

5. Remove meat, chicken and vegetables from broth. Discard herb bundle. Slice brisket and remove chicken from bones.

6. Meanwhile, cook potatoes in a large pot of boiling salted water for 20 minutes, or until tender. Drain. Cut potatoes in half if they are large.

7. Return meat, chicken, vegetables and potatoes to soup or serve as a main course and serve broth separately.

8. In a small bowl, combine mustard and mayonnaise and serve as a condiment.

Makes 8 servings

Salads

In the seventies and eighties, foodies would go to California for ideas and inspiration. Salads (main course and otherwise) were all the rage and practically all anyone was eating.

I never thought that trend would come to Canada—so cold and snowy for much of the year—but what did I know? I now serve salads before main courses, after them, beside them or even under them, with a piece of grilled meat, poultry or seafood served on a bed of greens (the old rule about not mixing hot and cold things on the plate seems to have gone out the window). I recycle leftovers like grilled vegetables into salads, and have even turned my favorite comfort food—mashed potatoes—into a Creole potato salad (page 53) full of spicy flavors and contrasting textures.

Meanwhile, salad dressings have become the new sauces. Vinaigrettes and dressings are simple and quick to make, and they can be used on much more than just greens. They make great marinades, sauces, drizzles for soups and main courses, and dips for appetizers.

Frisee with Roasted Pears and Caramelized Walnuts

This salad makes a perfect appetizer or light main course. The roasted pears and caramelized walnuts can be prepared ahead or, for a less time-consuming version, use raw pears and toasted walnuts.

Frisee is a type of endive with pale yellow and green leaves.

2 ripe but firm Bosc pears,
  cored and sliced or cut in wedges
1 tbsp (15 mL) brown sugar

Tarragon Mustard Dressing
2 tbsp (25 mL) sherry vinegar
  or red wine vinegar
1 tsp (5 mL) Dijon mustard
1 small clove garlic, minced
1/2 tsp (2 mL) salt
1/4 tsp (1 mL) pepper
1 tbsp (15 mL) chopped fresh
  tarragon, or 1/4 tsp (1 mL) dried
1/2 cup (125 mL) olive oil

Frisee Salad
3 cups (750 mL) frisee
  (about 3 oz/100 g)
2 Belgian endives,
  broken in pieces
1/2 cup (125 mL) crumbled
  blue cheese (mild Gorgonzola)
24 caramelized or toasted
  walnut halves

1. Arrange pears on a parchment-lined baking sheet. Sprinkle with brown sugar. Roast in a preheated 425 F (220 C) oven for 20 to 30 minutes, or until nicely browned.

2. Meanwhile, for dressing, in a small bowl, whisk together vinegar, mustard, garlic, salt, pepper and tarragon. Whisk in oil. Taste and adjust seasonings if necessary.

3. Place frisee and endives in a bowl. Arrange pears and crumbled cheese on top.

4. Just before serving, toss salad with dressing and sprinkle with walnuts.

Makes 4 to 6 servings

Caramelized Walnuts
In a small saucepan, stir together 1 cup (250 mL) granulated sugar and 3 tbsp (45 mL) water. Place on medium-high heat and cook, without stirring, until sugar dissolves and turns a golden caramel color. (Brush sugar down sides of pan with pastry brush dipped in cold water.) Remove immediately from heat and carefully transfer caramel to a heatproof bowl.

Caramel will be very hot, so be careful. Let cool just until caramel is thick enough to coat walnuts. If necessary, set bowl in a larger bowl of warm water to keep caramel liquid. Using a fork, skewer or large tweezers, dip each walnut in caramel and place on buttered waxed paper to set.

Makes 24

Rhonda's Grilled Vegetable Salad

Rhonda Caplan, who works with me, brought this salad dressing with iceberg lettuce for lunch every single day we taped my cooking show. It was comfort food for her because it was her mother's favorite dressing, and it was the first salad my son, Mark, would eat. Now we all love it.

This dressing tastes great on iceberg lettuce, but you can also serve it like this, with grilled vegetables and mixed salad greens (add grilled chicken or shrimp for a main course). You should have about 5 cups (1.25 L) chopped cooked vegetables in total.

Rice Vinegar Dressing

1/4 cup (50 mL) rice vinegar

1/2 tsp (2 mL) salt

Pinch pepper

1 clove garlic, minced

1/4 cup (50 mL) vegetable oil

2 green onions, finely chopped

3 tbsp (45 mL) shredded
   fresh basil

Grilled Vegetables

1 bulb fennel, trimmed and
   cut in wedges

1 Asian eggplant, trimmed
   and sliced lengthwise

1 red onion, thickly sliced

3 portobello mushrooms, trimmed
   and sliced

8 spears asparagus, trimmed

2 ears corn, husks and silk removed

2 tbsp (25 mL) olive oil or
   vegetable oil

1 tsp (5 mL) salt

1 sweet red pepper

1 sweet yellow pepper

8 cups (2 L) mixed salad greens

1. For dressing, in a small bowl, whisk together vinegar, salt, pepper and garlic. Whisk in oil. Stir in green onions and basil.

2. Brush fennel, eggplant, onion, mushrooms, asparagus and corn with oil and sprinkle with salt. (Use more oil if necessary.) Grill vegetables for a few minutes per side, or until browned. Grill peppers on all sides until blackened.

3. Rub skins off peppers and remove and discard cores and seeds. Dice peppers. Dice fennel, eggplant, onion, mushrooms and asparagus. Cut kernels off cobs (page 62).

4. In a large bowl, toss greens with grilled vegetables and dressing just before serving.

Makes 8 servings

Caesar Salad

Caesar salad may be the most popular salad ever. You can top it with cooked shrimp, sliced cooked chicken, crumbled cooked bacon, sliced hard-cooked eggs or chopped tomatoes; the dressing also makes a great dip or topping for a grilled chicken sandwich.

For a lighter version, omit the raw garlic and mayonnaise and add two heads pureed roasted garlic (page 116) to the dressing.

Caesar Dressing

1/4 cup (50 mL) mayonnaise

3 cloves garlic, minced

1 tsp (5 mL) anchovy paste,
  optional

1 tbsp (15 mL) lemon juice

1 tbsp (15 mL) red wine vinegar
  or sherry vinegar

1 tsp (5 mL) Dijon mustard

1 tsp (5 mL) Worcestershire sauce

1/2 cup (125 mL) olive oil,
  vegetable oil or a combination

3/4 cup (175 mL) grated
  Parmesan cheese

Salad

1 head Romaine lettuce, broken
  in pieces (about 8 cups/2 L)

2 cups (500 mL) croutons

2 oz (60 g) Parmesan cheese,
  thinly sliced

1. In a food processor, blender or bowl, combine mayonnaise, garlic, anchovy paste if using, lemon juice, vinegar, mustard and Worcestershire sauce. Whisk in olive oil. Blend in grated Parmesan. Taste and adjust seasonings if necessary.

2. Place lettuce in a large bowl. Pour dressing over lettuce and toss very well. Sprinkle with croutons and cheese slices.

Makes 4 to 6 servings

Homemade Croutons

Toss 2 cups (500 mL) bread cubes with 2 tbsp (25 mL) olive oil and 1/2 tsp (2 mL) salt. Sauté in a skillet for 5 minutes, or spread on a baking sheet and bake at 350 F (180 C) for 10 to 15 minutes, or until brown.

Creole Mashed Potato Salad

This potato salad is really different. The potatoes are coarsely mashed, the color is yellow and the flavor is wow. Creole mustard is a spicy coarse-grained mustard that is one of my favorite take-home foods from a trip to New Orleans. If you don't have it, just use grainy mustard. If you prefer less spice, use less mustard, less horseradish and much less hot red pepper sauce.

2 lb (1 kg) Yukon Gold or
  baking potatoes
3 eggs
1/4 cup (50 mL) mayonnaise
3 tbsp (45 mL) Creole mustard or
  coarse-grained mustard
2 tsp (10 mL) grated white
  horseradish
2 tsp (10 mL) hot red
  pepper sauce
1 1/2 tsp (7 mL) salt
2 stalks celery, thinly sliced on
  the diagonal
2 green onions, thinly sliced on
  the diagonal

1. Peel potatoes and cut into quarters. Place in a large saucepan of cold salted water and bring to a boil. Add eggs and cook for 10 minutes. Remove eggs and place in a bowl of cold water before peeling (shells will come off more easily). Continue cooking potatoes for 10 to 15 minutes, or until very tender. Drain potatoes and transfer to a large bowl.

2. Peel eggs. Separate yolks from whites. Dice hard-cooked egg whites.

3. In a small bowl, whisk together mayonnaise, mustard, horseradish, hot pepper sauce, salt and hard-cooked egg yolks. Mash mayonnaise mixture into potatoes.

4. Stir in diced egg whites and celery. Taste and adjust seasonings if necessary. Serve at room temperature sprinkled with green onions.

Makes 6 to 8 servings

Arugula Salad with Roasted Tomatoes and Olives

This is a vibrant salad with lots of different textures. Buy the best fresh Italian mozzarella that you can find and season the salad well. I like to break the cheese apart with my fingers rather than cut it, as it has a wonderful stringlike texture. Fresh lemon juice is a great alternative to balsamic vinegar, but if you have really good balsamic, use it in this recipe. (The better the balsamic, the less oil you will need.)

If you don't have time to roast the tomatoes, just use fresh cherry tomatoes instead.

4 plum tomatoes
 (about 1 lb/500 g)
4 tsp (20 mL) olive oil
1 tsp (5 mL) chopped
 fresh rosemary, or pinch dried
1 tsp (5 mL) chopped fresh thyme,
 or pinch dried
1 tsp (5 mL) salt
8 cups (2 L) arugula
 (about 6 oz/175 g)
8 oz (250 g) fresh buffalo
 mozzarella (bocconcini) or goat
 cheese
1/2 cup (125 mL) large black
 or green olives

Garlic Balsamic Dressing
2 tbsp (25 mL) balsamic vinegar
 or lemon juice
1 clove garlic, minced
1 tsp (5 mL) salt
1/4 tsp (1 mL) pepper
1/4 cup (50 mL) olive oil, or
 more to taste

1. Cut tomatoes in half crosswise. Trim bottoms so tomatoes can sit upright. Gently squeeze out seeds.

2. Place tomatoes cut side up on a parchment-lined baking sheet. Sprinkle with olive oil, rosemary, thyme and salt. Roast in a preheated 400 F (200 C) oven for 45 minutes, or until lightly browned. Cool.

3. If arugula leaves are large, break them in half. Arrange arugula on a serving platter. Top with tomatoes.

4. Gently break or cut cheese in pieces and add to salad (or place a piece of cheese on each tomato). Sprinkle with olives.

5. For dressing, in a small bowl, combine vinegar, garlic, salt and pepper. Whisk in oil. Taste and adjust seasonings if necessary.

6. Toss salad with dressing before serving.

Makes 6 to 8 servings

Roasted Asparagus, Beet and Goat Cheese Salad

Some people claim they do not like beets. But if you use organic beets and roast them, they are irresistible. In this salad I like to use a mild creamy goat cheese and some arugula in the mix of salad greens. You can use sugared walnuts (page 17) instead of plain toasted walnuts.

Walnut oil changes the personality of a salad dressing, adding a wonderful nutty flavor. I like to mix it with olive oil or vegetable oil so it won't taste too strong.

1 lb (500 g) beets

1 lb (500 g) asparagus or
  green beans, trimmed

1/2 tsp (2 mL) salt

Pinch pepper

1 tbsp (15 mL) olive oil

8 cups (2 L) mixed greens
  (about 8 oz/250 g)

4 oz (125 g) goat cheese,
  crumbled

1/2 cup (125 mL) toasted
  walnut halves

Walnut Oil Dressing

2 tbsp (25 mL) sherry vinegar
  or red wine vinegar

1 tsp (5 mL) salt

1/2 tsp (2 mL) Dijon mustard

1/4 cup (50 mL) walnut oil

2 tbsp (25 mL) olive oil, or
  more to taste

1. Trim beets and wrap in foil in a single layer. Bake in a preheated 400 F (200 C) oven for 1 to 1 1/2 hours, or until very tender. Unwrap and cool. Rub skins off beets and cut beets into wedges.

2. Meanwhile, arrange asparagus on a parchment-lined baking sheet. Sprinkle with salt, pepper and olive oil. Roast with beets for 10 to 15 minutes, or until lightly browned. Cool. Cut in half on the diagonal.

3. Place greens in a shallow salad bowl and top with asparagus, beets, goat cheese and walnuts.

4. In a small bowl, whisk vinegar with salt and mustard. Whisk in walnut oil and olive oil. Taste and adjust seasonings if necessary. Drizzle salad with dressing.

Makes 6 to 8 servings

Organic Food When Andrew Weil and Rosie Daley (authors of *The Healthy Kitchen*) came to the cooking school during their Toronto book tour, we decided to prepare a lunch according to Dr. Weil's principles of using healthful, fresh, all-natural ingredients. We used as many organic products as possible, including incredible greens from  David Cohlmeyer's Cookstown Greens, and everything was served on handmade wooden platters from Don Stinson in Tamworth, Ontario.

Andrew and Rosie loved the lunch (we served a version of the Salade Niçoise on page 59), and so did we. It was an amazing experience to eat a meal consisting only of the freshest natural ingredients, and to know exactly where every item had come from.

It is hard to eat like this every day. But we can pay more attention to where our food comes from and how it is produced. My philosophy on buying organic food is a mix of ideology and practicality. I want to support people who are growing and producing food without pesticides and harmful additives. And I would rather buy an organic apple with a few blemishes than a picture-perfect apple that has been subjected to several rounds of pesticides. So I buy organic whenever possible. We try to use only organic meat and poultry, we are very particular about our fish, and we buy organic greens as well as organic tofu and soy products. Organic products may not be available everywhere yet, but I do think it is the way of the future, and I look forward to it.

Salade Niçoise

This is the salad we served Andrew Weil and Rosie Daley when they came for lunch. We reinvent this every time we make it. Use green beans instead of asparagus, roasted red peppers instead of tomatoes, or try sweet potatoes or other root vegetables instead of potatoes. Serve it with the traditional canned tuna or with rare grilled tuna. (You can serve the tuna separately if you are entertaining vegetarian guests.)

Instead of grilling the asparagus, roast it in the oven for 10 to 15 minutes.

6 tbsp (90 mL) olive oil

2 tbsp (25 mL) chopped
  fresh rosemary, or pinch dried

1 tbsp (15 mL) salt

1 tbsp (15 mL) pepper

2 lb (1 kg) small potatoes,
  cleaned and halved

6 plum tomatoes, cut in quarters

1 lb (500 g) asparagus, trimmed

1 lb (500 g) tuna steak (sushi
  quality), 1 inch (2.5 cm) thick

10 cups (2.5 L) mixed greens
  or arugula

4 hard-cooked eggs

1/2 cup (125 mL) pitted
  black olives

Niçoise Dressing

1 clove garlic, minced

3 tbsp (45 mL) balsamic vinegar

1 tbsp (15 mL) lemon juice or
  sherry vinegar

1/2 cup (125 mL) olive oil

1/4 tsp (1 mL) salt

1/4 tsp (1 mL) pepper

2 tbsp (25 mL) chopped fresh
  tarragon or basil

1 small bunch chives,
  cut in 2-inch (5 cm) pieces

1. In a small bowl, combine olive oil, rosemary, salt and pepper.

2. Toss potatoes with half of oil mixture and spread on a parchment-lined baking sheet.

3. Arrange tomato wedges, skin side down, on a separate parchment-lined baking sheet.

4. Roast potatoes and tomatoes in a preheated 400 F (200 C) oven. Roast tomatoes for 35 to 45 minutes and potatoes for 45 to 60 minutes, or until brown.

5. Toss asparagus with seasoned oil mixture. Grill on barbecue or grill pan for 2 to 3 minutes, or until lightly browned.

6. Brush tuna with seasoned oil and grill for 2 minutes per side. Cool and slice thinly.

7. Arrange greens on a large platter. Arrange potatoes, tomatoes, tuna and asparagus on greens. Cut eggs into eighths, arrange around sides and sprinkle with olives.

8. For dressing, in a small bowl, blend garlic with vinegar, lemon juice, oil, salt, pepper and tarragon.

9. Drizzle salad with dressing and sprinkle with chives. Serve warm or at room temperature.

Grilled Mushroom and Asparagus Salad

Grilled mushrooms are meaty and succulent. This makes a fantastic appetizer, vegetarian main course or side dish.

The mushrooms can be sliced or left whole. Although wild mushrooms are usually stemmed, I like to use the trimmed portobello stems, too, as they contain lots of flavor. For a cleaner taste and look, I usually remove the gills. If you can't find shiitake and oyster mushrooms, just use more portobellos. The better the balsamic, the less oil you will need in the dressing.

12 oz (375 g) portobello
  mushrooms (about 3 large)
8 oz (250 g) fresh shiitake
  mushrooms, trimmed (12 to 16)
8 oz (250 g) oyster mushrooms,
  trimmed (12 to 16)
3 tbsp (45 mL) olive oil, divided
1/2 tsp (2 mL) salt, divided
1 onion, peeled
16 spears asparagus, trimmed and
  peeled if large (page 45)

Dressing
3 tbsp (45 mL) balsamic vinegar
1 tsp (5 mL) salt
1/2 tsp (2 mL) pepper
1 clove garlic, minced
3 tbsp (45 mL) olive oil, or
  more to taste
Handful fresh chives

1. Cut stems off portobellos. Trim stems and cut in half lengthwise. With a spoon, gently remove and discard gills underneath portobello mushroom caps. Combine all mushrooms in a bowl with 1 tbsp (15 mL) olive oil and 1/4 tsp (1 mL) salt.

2. Slice onion into thick rounds and brush with 1 tbsp (15 mL) olive oil and pinch of salt. Toss asparagus with remaining 1 tbsp (15 mL) olive oil and remaining pinch of salt.

3. Grill all vegetables for a few minutes on each side, or until lightly browned. Cut portobellos into quarters or thick slices. Cut shiitakes and oyster mushrooms in half. Cut onion slices in half. Cut asparagus spears in half on the diagonal. Combine vegetables in a large bowl.

4. In a small bowl, whisk together vinegar, salt, pepper and garlic. Whisk in olive oil. Taste and adjust seasonings and add oil if necessary. Toss vegetables with dressing. Cut chives into 2-inch (5 cm) pieces and sprinkle on top.

Makes 4 to 6 servings

Wheat Berry and Grilled Corn Salad

This is one of my favorite salads. It is somewhat exotic because of the chewy wheat berries (also called soft wheat kernels), but everyone loves it. You can vary the ingredients according to what you have on hand. Use rice instead of wheat berries, frozen corn instead of grilled corn (you should have about 3 cups/750 mL), cherry tomatoes instead of red peppers—the salad will still taste wonderful.

2 cups (500 mL) uncooked wheat
  berries
4 ears corn, husks and silk removed
2 sweet red peppers
8 oz (250 g) asparagus, trimmed

Orange Chipotle Dressing

1/2 cup (125 mL) rice vinegar
2 cloves garlic, minced
2 tbsp (25 mL) undiluted orange
  juice concentrate
1 tbsp (15 mL) minced chipotles or
  jalapeños, optional
1 tsp (5 mL) salt
1/2 tsp (2 mL) pepper
3 tbsp (45 mL) olive oil
1/2 cup (125 mL) chopped fresh
  cilantro
1/4 cup (50 mL) chopped fresh
  chives

1. Rinse wheat berries and place in a large saucepan. Cover with at least 4 inches (10 cm) cold water. Bring to a boil and simmer gently, covered, for 1 to 1 1/2 hours, or until tender. The wheat berries should still be chewy. Rinse with cold water and drain well. Place in a large bowl.

2. Meanwhile, grill corn until lightly browned all over, about 2 to 3 minutes. Cool. Cut corn in half. Place cut side down on a cutting board and, holding corn firmly, cut kernels off cob from top to bottom. Add corn to wheat berries.

3. Grill peppers on all sides until blackened. Cool. Remove skins and discard seeds and cores. Dice peppers. Add to wheat berries and corn.

4. Grill asparagus for a few minutes, or until barely cooked. Dice. Add to wheat berries. (Corn and peppers can also be used raw and asparagus can be steamed rather than grilled.)

5. For dressing, in a small bowl, combine vinegar, garlic, orange juice concentrate, chipotle if using, salt and pepper. Whisk in olive oil.

6. Toss salad with dressing and add herbs. Taste and adjust seasonings if necessary.

Makes 8 to 10 servings

Light Cooking

In the past ten years I have written three cookbooks in conjunction with the Heart and Stroke Foundation of Canada: *Simply HeartSmart, More HeartSmart* and *HeartSmart Cooking for Family and Friends*. During this  time I have had the opportunity to formulate my own ideas about eating for health, and I have actually changed the way I cook. I am a great believer in eating a large variety of foods and eating everything in moderation. I still love dessert, but I eat small portions made with only the best-quality ingredients.

Light Cooking Tips

- Cook with olive oil instead of butter where possible.
- Use less oil to start a recipe and use a nonstick pan.
- Omit or reduce whipping cream in soups and pasta sauces.
- Use sweeter vinegars in salad dressings so you will need less oil.
- Trim excess fat from meats. Use lean ground meat, chicken and turkey.
- Use lower-fat cooking methods such as roasting, poaching and grilling.
- Add flavor to dishes by using vinegars, herbs, spices and seasonings instead of adding fat.
- If you use strongly flavored cheese (e.g., old Cheddar), you won't need to use as much.
- Use whole eggs or egg whites instead of egg yolks where possible (1 whole egg = 2 yolks; 2 egg whites = 1 whole egg).
- Where possible, use yogurt cheese (page 23) instead of sour cream, whipping cream or mayonnaise.
- Use 1 percent or 2 percent milk.
- Toast nuts for maximum flavor; you will need less.

Grilled Calamari Salad with Cashews and Sesame

This recipe is inspired by a salad I had at Asia de Cuba in New York City. If you cut everything into bite-sized pieces, every mouthful will be bursting with contrasting flavors and textures.

If the calamari has not already been cut into fillets, open the sacs, rinse them and flatten them out. Score them lightly and hold them down as you grill (though you won't be able to completely stop them from curling up). You can also grill the squid whole and then cut it into rings.

Chicken, shrimp or steak can be used instead of calamari in this recipe.

Honey Sesame Dressing

1/4 cup (50 mL) orange juice

2 tbsp (25 mL) rice vinegar

1 tbsp (15 mL) honey

1 clove garlic, minced

1 tsp (5 mL) salt

1/3 cup (75 mL) vegetable oil

1 tsp (5 mL) roasted sesame oil

Salad

6 cups (1.5 L) coarsely
  chopped radicchio

6 cups (1.5 L) coarsely
  chopped curly endive

1 mango, peeled and diced

2 Asian pears, cored and diced

1 14-oz (398 mL) can hearts of
  palm, drained and diced

2 lb (1 kg) calamari (squid) fillets

2 tbsp (25 mL) roasted sesame oil

1 tsp (5 mL) salt

1/2 tsp (2 mL) pepper

1 ripe avocado

1/2 cup (125 mL) toasted cashews

1. For dressing, in a small bowl, whisk together orange juice, vinegar, honey, garlic and salt. Whisk in vegetable oil and sesame oil. Taste and adjust seasonings if necessary.

2. In a large bowl, toss radicchio and endive with mango, pears and hearts of palm.

3. Pat calamari very dry. Score lightly but do not cut through. Toss with sesame oil, salt and pepper. Grill for 1 minute per side on a barbecue, grill pan or skillet. Cut into bite-sized pieces.

4. Just before serving, peel and dice avocado and add to salad with cashews and calamari. Toss salad with dressing.

Makes 6 servings

Ripe Mango Salad with Peanut Dressing

My friend Lauren Gutter is a talented fashion designer, but her good taste does not stop with fabrics and clothing. She's a great cook and can spot a fashionable recipe a mile away. She came to me with an idea for a mango salad with peanut dressing, and this is what we concocted. Of course, we had to try it at least twenty times before we got it right—eating the mistakes, too (which were still pretty good).

Use mangoes that are ripe but still firm. If you are using coconut milk, pour any extra into a resealable heavy-duty plastic bag, freeze flat and just break off a piece when you need it.

Before using raw shallots, chop them and soak in ice water for 30 minutes to take out the sting.

Peanut Dressing

2 tbsp (25 mL) peanut butter

2 tbsp (25 mL) water

2 tbsp (25 mL) lime juice

1 tbsp (15 mL) fish sauce or
  soy sauce

1 tbsp (15 mL) granulated sugar

1/4 tsp (1 mL) hot Asian
  chile paste

2 tbsp (25 mL) coconut milk,
  optional

Salad

2 ripe mangoes

8 cups (2 L) mixed greens
  (about 8 oz/250 g)

1 tbsp (15 mL) finely chopped
  shallots

3/4 cup (175 mL) coarsely chopped
  toasted cashews or peanuts

1 tbsp (15 mL) chopped
  fresh cilantro

1. To make dressing, in a food processor, combine peanut butter, water, lime juice, fish sauce, sugar, chile paste and coconut milk if using. (If you are whisking by hand, combine peanut butter with water first to loosen it and then whisk in remaining ingredients.)

2. Peel mangoes. Cut flesh off pits and slice each mango into 8 wedges.

3. Arrange greens in a salad bowl. Top with mango.

4. Drizzle dressing over salad just before serving. Sprinkle with shallots, cashews and cilantro.

Makes 6 to 8 servings

Peeling Mango

To peel a mango easily, cut a small slice off the top and bottom (stem end). Stand the mango upright on cutting surface and slice off peel from top to bottom.

House Dressing

This variation on a basic vinaigrette is my favorite house dressing right now. The sweeter the vinegar, the less oil you will need.

This should provide enough dressing for 12 to 14 cups (3 to 3.5 L) salad greens. You could also add 1 tbsp (15 mL) chopped fresh herbs such as basil, chives, tarragon, parsley, cilantro or dill.

2 tbsp (25 mL) sherry vinegar
2 tbsp (25 mL) balsamic vinegar
1/2 tsp (2 mL) Dijon mustard
1/2 tsp (2 mL) salt
Pinch pepper
1 clove garlic, minced
1/3 cup (75 mL) olive oil
1/3 cup (75 mL) sunflower or canola oil

1. In a medium bowl, whisk together vinegars, mustard, salt, pepper and garlic. Gradually whisk in olive oil and sunflower oil. Taste and adjust seasonings if necessary.

Makes about 3/4 cup (175 mL)

Roasted Red Pepper Balsamic Dressing

The pureed peppers add a great texture to this low-fat dressing. You can use two bottled piquillo peppers (page 16) instead of roasting your own. The balsamic vinegar accentuates the sweetness of the peppers. Use this on greens, grain salads and pasta salads.

1 sweet red pepper
1 clove garlic, minced, or 1 head roasted garlic
   (page 116)
1/4 cup (50 mL) balsamic vinegar
1/2 tsp (2 mL) salt
1/2 tsp (2 mL) pepper
2 tbsp (25 mL) chopped fresh basil
2 tbsp (25 mL) olive oil
2 tbsp (25 mL) water

1. Cut pepper in half and remove seeds and core. Grill pepper under broiler, skin side up, until browned and blistered. Cool. Rub off skin.
2. In a food processor or blender, puree pepper with garlic, vinegar, salt, pepper, basil, oil and water. Taste and adjust seasonings if necessary.

Makes about 3/4 cup (175 mL)

Thousand Island Dressing

This old-fashioned dressing has stood the test of time. It is perfect in wraps, club sandwiches or even on burgers.

1 cup (250 mL) mayonnaise
1/4 cup (50 mL) chili sauce or ketchup
1 gherkin, finely chopped
1 tbsp (15 mL) granulated sugar
1 tbsp (15 mL) white vinegar
1/2 tsp (2 mL) paprika, optional

1. In a bowl, whisk together mayonnaise, chili sauce, gherkin, sugar, vinegar and paprika if using. Taste and adjust seasonings if necessary.

Makes 1 1/2 cups (375 mL)

Orange Chile Dressing

This is a great dressing for chicken, beef or salmon on greens. It can also be served as a dip with spring rolls or dumplings.

1 small clove garlic, minced
3 tbsp (45 mL) sweet Thai chile sauce,
    or 1 tsp (5 mL) hot Asian chile paste
1 tbsp (15 mL) undiluted orange juice concentrate
2 tbsp (25 mL) rice vinegar
1 tbsp (15 mL) soy sauce
2 tbsp (25 mL) olive oil
1 tsp (5 mL) roasted sesame oil

1. In a small bowl, combine garlic, chile sauce, orange juice concentrate, vinegar and soy sauce. Whisk in olive oil and sesame oil. Taste and adjust seasonings if necessary.

Makes 1/2 cup (125 mL)

Grilled Lemon Vinaigrette

Use this dressing on a green salad or, for a fabulous Greek potato salad, toss with 2 lb (1 kg) roasted potatoes (page 59). Grilling softens the lemon taste.

1 lemon, cut in half
1 clove garlic, minced
1 tsp (5 mL) salt
1/3 cup (75 mL) olive oil, approx.
1 tsp (5 mL) chopped fresh thyme or oregano

1. Place cut sides of lemon halves on a hot barbecue or grill pan. Grill for a couple of minutes, or until lemon is well browned. Cool.
2. Squeeze lemon juice into a bowl. Whisk in garlic and salt. Whisk in oil and thyme. Taste and adjust seasonings if necessary.

Makes about 1/2 cup (125 mL)

Sesame Miso Dressing

Miso is fermented soybean paste and is used in soups, dressings, dips and sauces. Light miso (blonde, white or yellow) is the lightest tasting and most versatile (the darker the miso, the stronger the flavor).

Use this as a salad dressing or as a topping for grilled fish. It also tastes great as a substitute for peanut dip (good for people who are allergic to peanuts, and the sesame oil is optional).

1/4 cup (50 mL) light miso paste
2 tbsp (25 mL) water
1 tbsp (15 mL) rice vinegar
1 tbsp (15 mL) soy sauce
1 tbsp (15 mL) brown sugar
2 tsp (10 mL) roasted sesame oil
1 tsp (5 mL) Dijon mustard
1 clove garlic, minced

1. In a bowl, combine miso, water, vinegar, soy sauce, brown sugar, sesame oil, Dijon and garlic. Taste and adjust seasonings if necessary.

Makes about 1/2 cup (125 mL)

Main Courses

Even though I cook a lot, I can still get a little frazzled when I entertain, so I always make sure I am very organized. I make lots of lists, and I plan the menu ahead. When you are cooking, it can be just as important to be a good organizer as a good cook.

When I am planning a dinner, I choose the main course first, since it is the meatiest part of the meal in every way—usually the biggest and most expensive menu item. If I decide on a simple main course, such as grilled meat or fish, then I go all out on the appetizer, side dishes and dessert. But if the main course is complicated, I usually keep the other elements very simple.

Your choice of main course will also depend on who you are entertaining. If you know your guests well, you can make something that requires last-minute preparation and the guests can hang around with you in the kitchen, or you can even put them to work helping! Otherwise, I like to stick to dishes that can be mostly prepared ahead.

Seafood Noodle Paella

When I was in Spain, I was surprised to see a kind of regional paella made with pasta instead of rice. The Spanish pasta is called fideos, but I use broken spaghetti.

This is an amazing party dish, and although you do not need to have a paella pan, it does look great when you bring it to the table.

6 tbsp (75 mL) olive oil, divided

1 lb (500 g) halibut, cod or
    monkfish, cut in chunks

1 lb (500 g) shrimp, with or
    without shells, cleaned

1 lb (500 g) squid fillets,
    cut in strips

1 tbsp (15 mL) salt, divided

1/2 tsp (2 mL) pepper

2 onions, chopped

3 cloves garlic, chopped

1 tsp (5 mL) paprika
    (preferably smoked)

1 sweet red pepper, peeled,
    seeded and diced

2 cups (500 mL) chopped
    canned tomatoes

6 cups (1.5 L) chicken stock or
    fish stock

1/4 tsp (1 mL) saffron threads

1 lb (500 g) dried spaghetti
    (or other long pasta), broken in
    1 1/2-inch (4 cm) pieces

16 mussels

2 tbsp (25 mL) chopped
    fresh parsley

1. Heat 2 tbsp (25 mL) olive oil in a large, deep ovenproof skillet on medium-high heat.

2. Season halibut, shrimp and squid with 1 tsp (5 mL) salt and pepper. Cook halibut and shrimp, separately, for about 2 minutes each. Cook squid for 30 seconds. Remove all seafood from skillet and reserve.

3. Return skillet to low heat and add 2 tbsp (25 mL) oil. Add onions and garlic and cook very gently for 5 minutes. Add paprika and red pepper and cook for 10 to 15 minutes, or until very tender. Add a little water if skillet becomes dry.

4. Add tomatoes, stock, remaining 2 tsp (10 mL) salt (depending on how salty the stock is) and saffron and bring to a boil. Add pasta. Cook, uncovered, for about 10 minutes, or until pasta is almost tender and liquid is almost completely absorbed.

5. Add partially cooked seafood. Place mussels on top. Drizzle with remaining 2 tbsp (25 mL) oil. Transfer to a preheated 425 F (220 C) oven for 15 to 20 minutes, or until all liquid is absorbed and pasta is turning crusty around edges. Sprinkle with parsley.

Makes 6 to 8 servings

Roasted Cod Adobo

When I visited London for the first time in ten years, I could not believe the difference in the food. It has become so sophisticated, so stylish, so good—and so expensive. This recipe was inspired by a lunch at The Eagle, a gastropub in the Clerkenwell area. It was recommended to me by Sue Henderson, a Toronto-based food stylist originally from London. The restaurant was so much fun and reasonably priced, and the food (and pints) were great.

You could also use salmon, haddock or halibut in this recipe.

1 clove garlic, finely chopped

1 tbsp (15 mL) ground cumin

1 tbsp (15 mL) paprika
(preferably smoked)

1 tsp (5 mL) salt

1 tsp (5 mL) pureed or dried
chipotles

1/2 tsp (2 mL) dried oregano

1/2 tsp (2 mL) dried thyme

2 tbsp (25 mL) chopped fresh
cilantro or parsley

2 tbsp (25 mL) olive oil

2 lb (1 kg) thick boneless
cod fillets, skin removed

1. In a small bowl, combine garlic, cumin, paprika, salt, chipotle, oregano, thyme, cilantro and oil.

2. Pat fish dry and smear with herb/spice mixture. Marinate for 20 minutes.

3. Place fish on a parchment-lined baking sheet. Roast in a preheated 425 F (220 C) oven for 15 to 20 minutes (or longer if fish is thicker than 1 inch/2.5 cm), or just until fish flakes.

Makes 6 servings

Roasted Salmon with Lemon Coriander Rub

Roasting is a fabulous no-fuss technique for cooking thick pieces of fish, and the result is juicy and moist. In this case the fish is coated with an East Indian-inspired rub. Serve it with mango salsa. It is also great without the salsa served at room temperature with Salade Niçoise (page 59).

1 tbsp (15 mL) paprika
  (preferably smoked)
1 tbsp (15 mL) grated lemon peel
1 tbsp (15 mL) crushed whole
  coriander seeds
1 tbsp (15 mL) granulated sugar
1 tbsp (15 mL) salt
1 tsp (5 mL) pepper
4 lb (2 kg) whole boneless
  salmon fillet, skin removed

1. In a small bowl, combine paprika, lemon peel, coriander, sugar, salt and pepper. Rub into fish.

2. Place fish on a large parchment-lined baking sheet and roast in a pre-heated 425 F (220 C) oven for 20 minutes, or just until fish flakes.

3. Transfer fish to a serving platter using two long spatulas.

Makes 8 to 10 servings

Mango Mint Salsa

Use this as a topping for grilled meat or fish. Add a diced tomato if you wish.

Peel 1 ripe mango. Cut fruit off pit and dice finely. Place in a medium bowl and toss with 1 diced roasted or raw sweet red pepper, 1 seeded and finely chopped jalapeño, 2 tbsp (25 mL) chopped fresh mint, 2 tbsp (25 mL) chopped fresh cilantro, 1 tbsp (15 mL) lime juice and 1/2 tsp (2 mL) salt.

Makes 1 1/2 cups (375 mL)

Sesame Salmon Burgers with Spicy Mayonnaise

You can make these burgers with swordfish, tuna, red snapper or halibut. The fresher the fish, the better the burger. If you do not have time to make the patties, just brush individual salmon fillets with the glaze and grill.

You can also serve these with wasabi mayonnaise (page 78).

1 lb (500 g) boneless salmon,
  skin removed, cut in chunks
2 egg whites
1/2 cup (125 mL) fresh
  breadcrumbs or panko
1/4 cup (50 mL) thick teriyaki
  sauce, divided
1 tsp (5 mL) salt
1 tbsp (15 mL) roasted sesame oil
2 tbsp (25 mL) sesame seeds

Spicy Mayonnaise
1/2 cup (125 mL) mayonnaise
2 tbsp (25 mL) sweet Thai chile
  sauce, or 1 tsp (5 mL)
  hot Asian chile paste

4 sesame buns, cut in half
  horizontally
16 thick slices English cucumber

1. Place fish in a food processor and chop finely. Add egg whites, breadcrumbs, 1 tbsp (15 mL) teriyaki sauce and salt. Blend together.

2. Lightly shape mixture into 4 patties about 1/2 inch (1 cm) thick (about 1/2 cup/125 mL each). Place patties on a baking sheet lined with waxed paper or parchment paper.

3. For glaze, in a small bowl, combine remaining 3 tbsp (45 mL) teriyaki sauce, sesame oil and sesame seeds.

4. In a separate small bowl, combine mayonnaise and sweet Thai sauce.

5. Grill burgers for 3 minutes per side. Brush with glaze, flip and cook for 2 minutes. Brush with glaze again, flip and cook for 2 minutes longer, or until cooked through. Do not overcook.

6. Place burgers on bottom halves of buns. Place 4 cucumber slices on each burger. Spread Spicy Mayonnaise on remaining halves of buns and top sandwiches.

Makes 4 servings

Teriyaki Sauce
In a small saucepan, combine 1/4 cup (50 mL) soy sauce, 1/4 cup (50 mL) water, 1/4 cup (50 mL) rice wine and 1/4 cup (50 mL) granulated sugar. Bring to a boil and simmer gently until reduced by half, or until thick and syrupy. Watch closely to make sure it does not burn or boil dry.

Makes about 1/2 cup (125 mL)

Grilled Salmon on Corn Salsa

The idea for this corn salsa came from Casa Bella, a charming restaurant in Gananoque, Ontario. You can barbecue or roast the salmon (if you are roasting it, leave the salmon in one piece and cut it into pieces before serving). A quirky tip I learned from Caprial Pence, owner of Caprial's Bistro in Portland, Oregon, to prevent fish from sticking to the grill is to spray it (the fish) with non-stick cooking spray. Don't try to turn it for at least a couple of minutes.

You can also make this with grilled scallops, shrimp or halibut. Serve warm or at room temperature.

6 ears corn, husks and silk removed

1 small red onion, thickly sliced

2 lb (1 kg) boneless salmon fillet, skin removed, cut in 6 pieces

2 tbsp (25 mL) olive oil

1 tsp (5 mL) salt

1/4 tsp (1 mL) pepper

1 bunch arugula, chopped (about 2 cups/500 mL packed)

Lime Chipotle Dressing

1 clove garlic, minced

2 tbsp (25 mL) lime juice

1 1/2 tsp (7 mL) salt

1 tbsp (15 mL) pureed chipotles

1/4 cup (50 mL) olive oil

1. Brush corn, onion and salmon with olive oil and sprinkle with salt and pepper. Barbecue salmon for about 5 minutes per side, or until just cooked. (Salmon can also be roasted on a parchment-lined baking sheet in a preheated 425 F/220 C oven for 15 minutes. Cut salmon into serving pieces after roasting.)

2. Barbecue onion and corn for a couple of minutes per side, until browned. Cool. Cut kernels off cobs into a large bowl (you should have about 4 cups/1 L). Dice onion and add to corn. Add arugula.

3. For dressing, in a small bowl, whisk together garlic, lime juice, salt and chipotles. Whisk in olive oil. Add to corn mixture and toss.

4. Arrange corn salsa on each plate. Top with a piece of salmon.

Makes 6 servings

Lime Cilantro Chutney

This is a delicious chutney for grilled fish or meat.

In a blender or food processor, chop 1 bunch fresh cilantro leaves and 1/2 cup (125 mL) fresh mint leaves. Add 3 tbsp (45 mL) lime juice, 1 seeded and chopped jalapeño, 1 tsp (5 mL) granulated sugar and 1/2 tsp (2 mL) salt and blend. Add up to 1/4 cup (50 mL) water to make a smooth puree.

Makes about 1/2 cup (125 mL)

Sesame Tuna Sandwiches with Asian Coleslaw

This great sandwich was served at the Four Seasons Hotel in Toronto, and when they took it off the menu I started making my own version. Buy sushi-grade high-quality tuna, as the inside should be slightly undercooked. Without the bun, this also makes a great carbohydrate-free main course with the wasabi mayonnaise drizzled on the tuna and topped with the coleslaw. Serve any extra coleslaw on the side.

The wasabi mayo is also great on hamburgers instead of ketchup and mustard.

4 tuna steaks, about 1/2 inch
   (1 cm) thick (4 oz/125 g each)
2 tbsp (25 mL) roasted sesame oil
2 tbsp (25 mL) coarsely
   ground pepper
2 tbsp (25 mL) sesame seeds
1 tbsp (15 mL) kosher salt

Wasabi Mayonnaise
1/4 cup (50 mL) mayonnaise
1 tbsp (15 mL) prepared wasabi,
   or to taste

Asian Coleslaw
4 cups (1 L) shredded Napa
   cabbage
1 carrot, grated
2 tbsp (25 mL) thinly sliced pickled
   ginger, slivered
2 green onions, thinly sliced
2 tbsp (25 mL) chopped
   fresh cilantro
1 clove garlic, minced
2 tbsp (25 mL) rice vinegar
2 tbsp (25 mL) soy sauce
2 tsp (10 mL) honey
1/2 tsp (2 mL) roasted sesame oil

4 sesame buns or focaccia buns,
   cut in half horizontally

1. Pat tuna dry. Rub with sesame oil.

2. In a small bowl, combine pepper, sesame seeds and salt. Sprinkle on tuna and pat in firmly. Marinate for 30 minutes.

3. In a small bowl, combine mayonnaise and wasabi until smooth.

4. To make coleslaw, in a large bowl, combine shredded cabbage, carrot, ginger, green onions and cilantro.

5. In a small bowl, combine garlic, rice vinegar, soy sauce, honey and sesame oil. Toss cabbage with dressing.

6. Grill tuna for 1 1/2 to 2 minutes per side. Fish should be charred outside and rare inside.

7. Assemble sandwich by spreading bottom halves of buns with a spoonful of wasabi. Top with tuna, coleslaw and top halves of buns.

Makes 4 sandwiches

Wasabi

Wasabi looks like a small, pale-green ginger root. It is grated like horseradish and used as a condiment and seasoning in Japanese dishes. You can buy it in powdered or paste form (it is sometimes also available fresh). Powdered wasabi will lose its heat if it is mixed with water too far in advance, so if you make it ahead, stir it vigorously just before using.

Kung Pao Shrimp with Cashews

Black bean sauce is a pungent flavoring sauce made with fermented and salted black beans. It is used in small quantities in Asian dishes as a seasoning in stir-fries, marinades and glazes. I like Lee Kum Kee black bean sauce. Store it in the refrigerator once the jar has been opened.

This is great made with shrimp or chicken.

Shrimp

1 lb (500 g) extra-large cleaned
  shrimp (about 20)

4 tsp (20 mL) soy sauce

1 tsp (5 mL) granulated sugar

1 tsp (5 mL) roasted sesame oil

Sauce

2 tbsp (25 mL) soy sauce

2 tbsp (25 mL) black bean sauce

1 tbsp (15 mL) granulated sugar

2 tsp (10 mL) roasted sesame oil

1/4 cup (50 mL) water, divided

1 tsp (5 mL) cornstarch

3 tbsp (45 mL) vegetable oil,
  divided

2 cloves garlic, chopped

1 tbsp (15 mL) chopped
  fresh ginger

1/2 tsp (2 mL) hot Asian
  chile paste

1 sweet red pepper, seeded and
  cut in 1-inch (2.5 cm) cubes

1 cup (250 mL) frozen shelled
  edamame (fresh soy beans)
  or peas

3 green onions, sliced on the
  diagonal

1/2 cup (125 mL) toasted cashews

1. In a large bowl, combine shrimp, soy sauce, sugar and sesame oil. Marinate for 20 minutes.

2. For sauce, in a small bowl, combine soy sauce, black bean sauce, sugar, sesame oil and 2 tbsp (25 mL) water.

3. In a small bowl, combine remaining 2 tbsp (25 L) water and cornstarch until smooth.

4. To cook, heat 2 tbsp (25 mL) oil in a large nonstick skillet or wok on medium-high heat. Add shrimp and stir-fry until lightly browned, about 1 to 2 minutes. Remove shrimp from pan and reserve. Wipe pan clean.

5. Heat remaining 1 tbsp (15 mL) oil in skillet. Add garlic, ginger and chile paste. Stir-fry for 30 seconds. Add red pepper. Stir-fry for 1 to 2 minutes, or until pepper softens slightly.

6. Add sauce mixture to skillet and cook for 1 minute.

7. Add edamame and shrimp. Stir in cornstarch mixture. Cook for 30 seconds, or until sauce thickens slightly. Add green onions and cook for 30 seconds. Sprinkle with cashews.

Makes 4 to 6 servings

Pecan-crusted Tilapia with Lemon Butter

This is a simplified and lower-fat version of a delicious dish I had in Lafayette, Louisiana. I like to brown the fish on top of the stove and finish it in the oven to prevent the nuts from burning and keep the fish from drying out. This double-cooking technique is a great way to cook fish.

Tilapia is a thin, white-fleshed, light-tasting fish. If you can't find it, use red snapper fillets. This would also work well with flattened boneless chicken breasts.

1 tbsp (15 mL) paprika
   (preferably smoked)
1 tsp (5 mL) salt
1/2 tsp (2 mL) pepper
1/2 cup (125 mL) all-purpose flour
2 eggs
1 tsp (5 mL) hot red pepper sauce
1 1/2 cups (375 mL) finely
   chopped pecans
3/4 cup (175 mL) dry
   breadcrumbs or panko
2 lb (1 kg) tilapia fillets (6 pieces)
3 tbsp (45 mL) vegetable oil,
   or more

Lemon Butter Sauce
2 tbsp (25 mL) butter
2 tbsp (25 mL) lemon juice
1 tbsp (15 mL) Worcestershire
   sauce
1 tsp (5 mL) hot red pepper sauce

1. In a shallow dish, combine paprika, salt, pepper and flour. In a separate shallow dish, beat eggs with hot pepper sauce. Combine nuts and breadcrumbs in third dish.

2. Pat fish dry. Dip fish into flour mixture and shake off excess. Dip into egg mixture and then pat in breadcrumb/nut mixture. Arrange on a parchment-lined baking sheet and refrigerate until ready to cook.

3. Heat oil in a large skillet on medium-high heat. Cook fish in two batches for 1 to 2 minutes per side, or until browned. Use additional oil if necessary. Place fish on a foil-lined baking sheet in a single layer.

4. Transfer fish to a preheated 400 F (200 C) oven and bake for 6 to 10 minutes, or until fish flakes easily.

5. Meanwhile, wipe skillet and return to heat to make sauce. Add butter, lemon juice, Worcestershire and hot pepper sauce. Bring to a boil. Spoon sauce on top of fish.

Makes 6 servings

Cooking for Children

As a child I was an extremely fussy eater. If I saw a tomato on my plate in a restaurant (tomatoes were the only garnish back then), I couldn't eat anything else on the plate, and if my mom sent the plate back and they removed the offending tomato without cleaning  the plate, that was just as bad, because a tomato had been there once! But my mother had infinite patience, and she understood that children have a different sense of taste and texture.

When I hear parents say that their kids just have to try one bite of something before they can leave the table, I often think of my first trip to Asia, where I was served things that other people ate all the time, but they were not things that I could eat even one bite of.

Kids usually enjoy lunches and dinners that are familiar; it's something they can count on in a world that is always changing. My kids both took peanut butter sandwiches for lunch for at least ten years. When my son was about eight, I gave him a cheese sandwich one day and when he came home from school he put his little hands on his little hips and told me that when he wanted a change he would ask for it. (And all this time I appeared on *Canada AM* every September, telling parents how to make school lunches interesting!)

My kids were always "selective" eaters. My mom said it was payback time. So I learned to cook dinners in layers. I wasn't prepared to make three different dinners the way my mom did, but I would cook something I could serve plain for the kids and then I would dress it up for Ray and me.

For example, if I made pasta, I would have one pot with the pasta, another pot with the tomato sauce and a skillet with sautéed chicken and vegetables. My daughter would have plain pasta, my son would have pasta and tomato sauce, and Ray and I would have everything. You can do this with pizza, sandwiches, stir-fries and even grilled chicken or steak with sauces and various veggies. That way you keep everyone happy.

Usually.

Angelhair Pasta with Tomato Cream Sauce

This is a sure winner with kids and adults. It is my basic all-purpose tomato sauce with a bit of cream. (The cream can be omitted and it is still delicious.) Kids love the thin angelhair noodles (sometimes called capellini), but it cooks very quickly so be careful not to overcook it. You can also use spaghettini, but it will take a bit longer to cook. (Most pasta manufacturers don't even recommend cooking times. The only way to tell whether pasta is ready is to taste it; it should be cooked through but still firm.)

To dress this up for grownups, I like to top each serving with grilled shrimp (page 3) and dot with pesto.

1 tbsp (15 mL) olive oil

1 small onion, chopped

1 clove garlic, finely chopped

2 cups (500 mL) pureed fresh
  or canned tomatoes

1 tsp (5 mL) salt

1/4 tsp (1 mL) pepper

1/2 cup (125 mL) whipping cream,
  optional

3/4 lb (375 g) dried angelhair pasta

2 tbsp (25 mL) butter, optional

1/2 cup (125 mL) grated
  Parmesan cheese

1. Heat olive oil in a large deep skillet on medium heat. Add onion and garlic and cook gently for a few minutes until tender, but do not brown. Add tomatoes and bring to a boil. Add salt and pepper. Cook gently for about 5 minutes, or until thick. Taste and adjust seasonings if necessary.

2. Add cream if using and simmer gently for 3 minutes.

3. Meanwhile, cook angelhair pasta in a large pot of boiling salted water for 2 to 3 minutes, or just until tender. Drain well. Toss with butter if using and add to sauce in skillet. Toss over very low heat for 1 minute. If sauce is too thick, add a little pasta-cooking liquid.

4. Serve with grated Parmesan.

Makes 4 to 6 servings

Pasta Pot

I love to use a pasta pot to cook pasta. It's a large pot with a second pot that fits inside and looks like a colander. You just lift out the inside pot and the pasta automatically drains. These pots are also great for making stock (you don't have to strain it; just lift out the bones and vegetables), or cooking potatoes.

Pesto

In a food processor, combine 2 cups (500 mL) fresh basil leaves, 1/2 cup (125 mL) fresh parsley, 2 cloves garlic, 1/3 cup (75 mL) toasted pine nuts, 1/2 tsp (2 mL) salt and 1/4 tsp (1 mL) pepper. Combine with on/off pulses until finely chopped. Add 1/2 cup (125 mL) olive oil and puree. Freeze. Before using, stir in 1/2 cup (125 mL) grated Parmesan cheese.

Makes about 1 cup (250 mL).

Jenny's Macaroni and Cheese

Jenny Burke, who works with me at the cooking school, is an artist in everything she does. She is a person who thinks with every part of her brain—she is mathematical as well as artistic, and she is an amazing cook. Her daughter Ashley was a very selective eater when she was younger, and Jenny and I often compared notes about what to serve kids. Here is Jenny's version of macaroni and cheese. Add the veggies your kids like.

Use old Cheddar cheese in this recipe for the most flavor.

2 cups (500 mL) dried penne
   (about 1/2 lb/250 g)
2 cups (500 mL) cauliflower florets
2 cups (500 mL) broccoli florets
2 tbsp (25 mL) butter
1 small onion, chopped
3 tbsp (45 mL) all-purpose flour
2 1/2 cups (625 mL) milk
1 tsp (5 mL) salt
3 cups (750 mL) grated old
   Cheddar cheese, (about
   12 oz/375 g) divided
1/2 cup (125 mL) fresh
   breadcrumbs or panko

1. Add pasta to a large pot of boiling salted water and cook for 4 to 5 minutes, or just until pasta is beginning to soften. Add cauliflower and cook for 4 minutes longer. Add broccoli and continue to cook for 4 minutes, or until pasta is completely cooked.

2. Meanwhile, in a large deep skillet, melt butter on medium-high heat. Add onion and cook until tender and fragrant, about 2 minutes.

3. Reduce heat. Sprinkle flour over onions and cook for 1 to 2 minutes on gentle heat until flour is lightly browned. Whisk in milk and salt. Bring to a boil and cook for 5 minutes.

4. In a small bowl, combine 1/2 cup (125 mL) cheese and breadcrumbs.

5. Add remaining 2 1/2 cups (625 mL) cheese to sauce. Cook gently for 2 to 3 minutes, or until cheese melts.

6. Drain pasta and vegetables well and add to sauce. Combine. Transfer pasta mixture to a lightly oiled 13- x 9-inch (3 L) baking dish. Sprinkle cheese and breadcrumb mixture on top.

7. Bake in a preheated 350 F (180 C) oven for 20 to 30 minutes, or until crispy and bubbling.

Makes 6 to 8 servings

Macaroni and Cheese with Roasted Vegetables
Peel about 2 lb (1 kg) root vegetables (e.g., squash, celeriac, parsnips, sweet potatoes, etc.) and cut into bite-sized chunks. Toss vegetables with a little olive oil, salt and dried thyme and spread on a parchment-lined baking sheet. Roast at 400 F (200 C) for 45 to 50 minutes, or until brown and tender. Add to drained pasta and sauce in place of cauliflower and broccoli.

Wild Mushroom Lasagna

When I was at the market in Barcelona, I saw so many different varieties of wild mushrooms, some of which I had never seen before. It made me want to cook right then, but as there was no kitchen in our tiny hotel room, I had to wait until I got home. Although the same mushrooms aren't available here, this lasagna satisfies my mushroom cravings. Use any edible wild mushrooms that you find in your market, or combine with cultivated mushrooms to keep the cost down.

This is a great vegetarian main course; it can be made ahead and even frozen.

1/4 cup (50 mL) olive oil

4 cloves garlic, finely chopped

2 shallots, finely chopped

2 lb (1 kg) wild mushrooms, trimmed and sliced

1 tsp (5 mL) salt

1/2 tsp (2 mL) pepper

2 tbsp (25 mL) chopped fresh parsley

Sauce

1/3 cup (75 mL) butter

1/2 cup (125 mL) all-purpose flour

5 cups (1.25 L) milk, hot

2 tsp (10 mL) salt

1/2 tsp (2 mL) pepper

Pinch grated nutmeg

1 lb (500 g) dried lasagna noodles

1 1/2 cups (375 mL) grated Parmesan cheese

2 tbsp (25 mL) butter, cut in bits

1. Heat olive oil in a large skillet on medium heat. Add garlic and shallots and cook gently until very fragrant, about 3 minutes. Add mushrooms and cook on high heat for 15 minutes, or until any liquid evaporates. Stir in salt, pepper and parsley.

2. Heat butter in a large saucepan on medium heat. Add flour and cook for a few minutes, but do not brown. Whisk in milk and bring to a boil. Add salt, pepper and nutmeg.

3. Meanwhile, in a large deep skillet or Dutch oven of boiling salted water, cook lasagna noodles, about three at a time, for about 5 minutes (or according to package directions), or until just tender. Rinse in a large bowl of ice water and arrange on baking sheets lined with tea towels.

4. To assemble, butter a 13- x 9-inch (3 L) baking dish. Arrange a single layer of lasagna noodles in bottom. Spread some sauce over noodles. Dot with some mushrooms. Sprinkle with some Parmesan. Repeat, using 4 layers of noodles. Top with sauce and cheese and dot with butter.

5. Bake in a preheated 400 F (200 C) oven for 30 to 35 minutes, or until browned and bubbly. Let rest for 10 minutes before serving.

Makes 8 servings

Penne with Braised Escarole and Pancetta

This is a take-off on a wonderful pasta dish I had at Lupa, one of Mario Batalli's restaurants in New York. Because it was my friend's meal and not mine, I only had a taste, so when I got home I made it for myself. This isn't quite the same as Mario's, of course, but it's still pretty good.

Escarole is a sturdy lettuce that's great for cooking. If you can't find it, use Swiss chard.

1 tbsp (15 mL) olive oil

4 oz (125 g) thickly sliced pancetta
   or bacon, diced

1 onion, chopped

3 cloves garlic, finely chopped

Pinch hot red pepper flakes

1 large bunch escarole
   (about 12 oz/375 g),
   trimmed and chopped
   (8 cups/2 L packed)

1 cup (250 mL) chicken stock

2 tsp (10 mL) salt

1/2 tsp (2 mL) pepper

2 tbsp (25 mL) butter or olive oil

1 1/2 cups (375 mL) diced crusty
   bread

3/4 lb (375 g) dried penne

1. Heat olive oil in a large deep skillet or Dutch oven on medium-high heat. Add pancetta and cook for a couple of minutes until crisp. Remove pancetta from pan and reserve.

2. Discard all but 2 tbsp (25 mL) fat in pan. Add onion, garlic and hot pepper flakes. Cook for a few minutes just until tender and fragrant.

3. Add escarole and cook for a few minutes until wilted. Add chicken stock, salt and pepper and remove from heat.

4. In a separate skillet, melt butter on medium-high heat. Add bread cubes. Cook, stirring, for 2 to 3 minutes, or until lightly browned and crisp. Drain on paper towels and reserve.

5. Meanwhile, cook pasta in a large pot of boiling salted water for 10 to 12 minutes, or until just tender. Drain pasta and add to sauce. Toss well and cook gently for a few minutes until liquid is absorbed and sauce coats pasta. Sprinkle with pancetta and bread cubes and toss.

Makes 6 servings

Baked Chicken with Basil Breadcrumbs

When my kids were growing up, I could never have too many chicken recipes. This one was and still is a winner. Use fresh breadcrumbs or panko.

Leaving the skin on the chicken breasts will keep them juicier, but you can remove the skin if you prefer. This topping also works with salmon or halibut. If you are using boneless, skinless chicken breasts, cook them for about 15 minutes.

1 clove garlic, chopped

1/2 cup (125 mL) chopped
  fresh basil or parsley

1 1/2 cups (375 mL) fresh
  breadcrumbs or panko

2 tsp (10 mL) salt

1/2 tsp (2 mL) pepper

2 tbsp (25 mL) olive oil

2 tbsp (25 mL) butter or
  additional olive oil

6 single chicken breasts, bone in,
  with skin on

1. Combine garlic, basil, breadcrumbs, salt and pepper in a food processor until finely chopped. Add oil and butter and process with on/off pulses until mixture is moist but not paste-like.

2. Arrange chicken on a parchment-lined baking sheet. Pat about 1/4 cup (50 mL) breadcrumb mixture onto top of each chicken breast.

3. Bake in a preheated 375 F (190 C) oven for 30 to 40 minutes, or until chicken is cooked through but still juicy. (Don't worry if a little of the breadcrumb mixture falls off.)

Makes 6 servings

Breadcrumbs

My favorite commercial breadcrumbs are panko. These are the breadcrumbs that the fast-food industry uses to make foods really crisp. They are made with only the whites of the bread and the crumbs come in large shards. I use them whenever I want dry or fresh breadcrumbs.

If you can't find panko, make your own breadcrumbs. They will still be infinitely better than the dust you find on most store shelves.

To make fresh breadcrumbs, process fresh bread chunks in a food processor until you have coarse crumbs. Store these in the freezer.

To make dry breadcrumbs, spread fresh breadcrumbs on a baking sheet and bake at 350 F (180 C) for 5 to 10 minutes, or until lightly browned and completely dry. Process until fine and store in a tightly sealed container at room temperature or freeze.

Breaded Chicken Cutlets

This is a family favorite. Make it as cutlets or chicken fingers and serve it plain or with tomato sauce. Use more breadcrumbs instead of cornflake crumbs if you wish. For a lighter version, arrange the cutlets in a single layer on a lightly oiled baking sheet and bake at 375 F (190 C) for 20 minutes, or until cooked through.

1 1/2 lb (750 g) boneless skinless
  chicken breasts
1 tsp (5 mL) salt
1 cup (250 mL) all-purpose flour
2 eggs
1 1/2 cups (375 mL) dry
  breadcrumbs or panko
1 1/2 cups (375 mL) cornflake
  crumbs
1/4 cup (50 mL) vegetable oil
1 lemon

1. Cut open one side of a large heavy-duty resealable plastic bag. Place chicken pieces in bag one at a time and pound thin with a meat pounder. (You can also pound the chicken between sheets of waxed paper, but the heavy plastic will not rip as easily.) Sprinkle chicken pieces with salt.

2. Place flour in a shallow dish. Beat eggs in another shallow dish. Mix breadcrumbs with cornflake crumbs in a third dish.

3. Dip chicken pieces into flour and shake off excess. Dip them into eggs and allow excess to drip off. Then pat breadcrumbs in firmly. Arrange chicken on a rack set over a baking sheet to dry. If not cooking right away, refrigerate.

4. To cook, heat oil in a large skillet on medium-high heat. Cook chicken in batches for a few minutes per side, or until browned. If you have to add more oil, add it between batches and heat before cooking chicken. The cutlets will cook quickly as they are very thin. Drain on paper towels.

5. Squeeze half of lemon over cutlets. Slice remaining lemon and use as a garnish.

Makes 4 to 6 servings

Chicken Parmesan

Arrange cooked breaded chicken cutlets on a baking sheet in a single layer. Drizzle with 1 1/2 cups (375 mL) tomato sauce (page 83). Arrange 8 oz (250 g) thinly sliced mozzarella on top and sprinkle with 1/4 cup (50 L) grated Parmesan cheese. Bake at 350 F (180 C) for 15 to 20 minutes. Sprinkle with 2 tbsp (25 mL) shredded fresh basil before serving.

Southwest Chicken Parmesan

Arrange cooked breaded chicken cutlets on a baking sheet in a single layer. Drizzle with 1 1/2 cups (375 mL) Smoky Tomato Sauce (page 90). Arrange 8 oz (250 g) thinly sliced smoked mozzarella on top and sprinkle with 1/4 cup (50 mL) grated Parmesan cheese. Bake at 350 F (180 C) for 20 minutes. Sprinkle with 2 tbsp (25 mL) chopped fresh cilantro before serving.

Chicken Meatloaf with Smoky Tomato Sauce

I never liked meatloaf when I was a kid, but I am making up for it now. I love this updated version made with ground chicken and a smoky, spicy tomato sauce, but you can make an old-fashioned version instead. I serve it without the sauce for kids (some will eat it and some are waiting until they grow up) and with the sauce for adults.

1 tbsp (15 mL) olive oil

1 onion, chopped

2 cloves garlic, finely chopped

2 lb (1 kg) ground chicken

2 eggs

2 tsp (10 mL) salt

1/2 tsp (2 mL) pepper

1/2 tsp (2 mL) hot Asian
  chile paste, optional

1 tbsp (15 mL) Worcestershire
  sauce

1 tbsp (15 mL) Dijon mustard

2/3 cup (150 mL) ketchup, divided

1 cup (250 mL) fresh
  breadcrumbs or panko

2 tbsp (25 mL) chopped
  fresh parsley

Smoky Tomato Sauce

1 tbsp (15 mL) olive oil

1 onion, chopped

3 cloves garlic, finely chopped

1 tsp (5 mL) pureed chipotles,
  or more to taste

3 cups (750 mL) chopped fresh
  tomatoes, or one 28-oz (796 mL)
  can plum tomatoes, with juices

1 tsp (5 mL) salt

1/2 tsp (2 mL) pepper

2 tbsp (25 mL) chopped
  fresh cilantro

1. Heat oil in a large nonstick skillet on medium heat. Add onion and garlic and cook gently for a few minutes, or until tender and fragrant. Cool.

2. In a large bowl, combine chicken, eggs, salt, pepper, chile paste if using, Worcestershire, mustard, 1/2 cup (125 mL) ketchup, breadcrumbs, parsley and onion mixture. Knead together.

3. Place mixture in a 9- x 5-inch (2 L) parchment- or foil-lined loaf pan. Cover with parchment or foil. Bake in a preheated 350 F (180 C) oven for 1 hour. Uncover, brush with remaining 2 tbsp (25 mL) ketchup and bake for 30 minutes longer. Drain off any juices and let sit for 5 minutes before unmolding.

4. Meanwhile, to make sauce, heat oil in a large deep skillet on medium-high heat. Add onion and garlic and cook for a few minutes until tender. Add chipotles and cook for 30 seconds. Add tomatoes, salt and pepper and bring to a boil. Cook gently for 15 minutes, or until thick. Puree. Taste and adjust seasonings if necessary.

5. Slice meatloaf and serve with sauce. Sprinkle with cilantro.

Makes 8 servings

Old-fashioned Meatloaf

Instead of ground chicken, use ground beef, ground veal, or a combination. Omit the chipotles and cilantro in the sauce.

Coconut Pepper Chicken

I was lucky enough to travel to India with Meena Patak, the driving force behind the Patak empire of Indian foods. She is a wonderful cook and described a recipe like this for my column in the *National Post*. I served it with a fabulous rice pilaf (page 126) in a class featuring a holiday buffet, and everyone reported back that their friends and families loved it—even those who didn't think they liked curry.

Freeze any leftover coconut milk to use another time.

1 tbsp (15 mL) ground coriander

1 tbsp (15 mL) ground cumin

2 tsp (10 mL) coarsely ground
  black pepper

1 tsp (5 mL) salt

1/2 tsp (2 mL) turmeric

1/2 tsp (2 mL) cayenne

2 lb (1 kg) boneless skinless
  chicken pieces (cut each breast
  into 4 pieces)

2 tbsp (25 mL) vegetable oil

1 large onion, chopped

2 cloves garlic, finely chopped

1 tbsp (15 mL) chopped
  fresh ginger

1 jalapeño or serrano, seeded and
  chopped

1 cup (250 mL) pureed
  canned tomatoes

1/2 cup (125 mL) coconut milk

2 tbsp (25 mL) chopped salted
  shelled pistachios

1/4 cup (50 mL) fresh
  cilantro leaves

1. In a large bowl, combine coriander, cumin, pepper, salt, turmeric and cayenne.

2. Pat chicken pieces dry. Toss chicken with spices. Marinate for 15 minutes or refrigerate overnight.

3. Heat oil in a large deep skillet on medium-high heat. Add onion and cook for 15 minutes, or until browned. Add garlic, ginger and jalapeño. Cook for 5 minutes. Add chicken and cook for 5 minutes, or until lightly browned.

4. Add tomatoes and bring to a boil. Reduce heat, cover and simmer gently for 10 minutes.

5. Add coconut milk, cover and cook for 5 minutes longer. Sprinkle chicken with pistachios and cilantro.

Makes 6 to 8 servings

Grilled Chicken Sandwiches with Charmoula

When my kids were little, I discovered charmoula, a wonderful Moroccan-flavored mayonnaise. I used it on salads, as a dip and, finally, as a sauce for grilled chicken sandwiches. Everyone went wild for them, and my kids started to make plans to open Bonnie's Sandwich Shack. At first I thought it was a joke, but when they found a location I realized my husband was in on it, too, and I started getting scared. So I nixed the plan.

The charmoula is also wonderful on burgers and satays.

Charmoula Mayo

1/2 cup (125 mL) mayonnaise

2 cloves garlic, minced

1/2 tsp (2 mL) ground cumin

1 tsp (5 mL) paprika
  (preferably smoked)

1/4 tsp (1 mL) cayenne

1 tbsp (15 mL) lemon juice

1/4 cup (50 mL) chopped
  fresh cilantro

Sandwiches

4 single boneless, skinless
  chicken breasts
  (about 1 1/2 lb/750 g total)

1 tsp (5 mL) paprika
  (preferably smoked)

1 tsp (5 mL) brown sugar

1 tsp (5 mL) grated lemon peel

1 tsp (5 mL) salt

1/4 tsp (1 mL) pepper

1 onion, cut in 4 thick slices

1 tbsp (15 mL) olive oil

1 sweet red pepper, halved,
  cored and seeded

4 focaccia buns or kaiser rolls,
  cut in half horizontally

4 leaves lettuce

1. For charmoula mayo, in a small bowl, combine mayonnaise, garlic, cumin, paprika, cayenne, lemon juice and cilantro.

2. Remove "filets" from chicken breasts and save for chicken fingers or stir-fries. Pound remaining chicken breasts so they are an even thickness.

3. In a small bowl, combine paprika, brown sugar, lemon peel, salt and pepper. Rub into chicken on both sides.

4. Brush chicken and onion slices with olive oil. Grill chicken for about 3 to 4 minutes per side, or until just cooked through. Grill onion slices for 2 to 3 minutes per side, or until tender. Grill peppers skin side down for about 5 minutes, or until charred. Rub skins off peppers and cut each piece in half.

5. Place chicken on bottom halves of buns. Top with onions and red peppers. Arrange lettuce on top. Spread mayo on top bun and sandwich together.

Makes 4 servings

Grilled Chicken Club Sandwiches
with Avocado Mayonnaise
This is a fabulous variation of a club sandwich. You can also make it in a tortilla, roll it up and grill it.

Instead of the avocado mayonnaise, you could use wasabi (page 78) or charmoula mayo (page 93).

4 single boneless, skinless
  chicken breasts
  (about 1 1/2 lb/750 g total)
1 tsp (5 mL) salt
1/2 tsp (2 mL) pepper
1 tbsp (15 mL) olive oil
1 ripe avocado
1/2 cup (125 mL) mayonnaise
1/4 cup (50 mL) chopped
  fresh cilantro
8 thin slices sourdough bread
4 thin slices tomato
4 slices Monterey Jack or
  smoked mozzarella cheese
4 slices bacon, cooked and
  cut in half
4 tsp (20 mL) melted butter
  or olive oil

1. Place chicken breasts, one at a time, in a heavy plastic bag or between pieces of parchment paper and pound until very thin.

2. In a small bowl, combine salt, pepper and olive oil. Rub into chicken. Grill on a hot barbecue or grill pan for 3 to 4 minutes per side, depending on thickness, or until cooked.

3. To make mayonnaise, cut avocado in half and remove pit. Scoop out flesh. Combine avocado and mayonnaise. Mash in a bowl or puree in a food processor. Stir in cilantro.

4. Spread 4 slices of bread with avocado mayonnaise. Top with chicken, tomato, cheese and bacon. Add top slice of bread and press firmly. Brush outside of sandwich with melted butter.

5. Just before serving, grill sandwiches for a few minutes on both sides on a hot barbecue or grill pan or in a sandwich maker until grill marks are on bread and cheese melts. As sandwiches cook, press firmly with a heavy spatula to compress.

Makes 4 sandwiches

Grilled Chicken with Cashews and Garlic

One of my favorite restaurants in Vancouver is Vij's. The food has twice the flavor of that of many other restaurants, so it is no wonder it is always busy. The warm welcome you receive from Vikram Vij is worth the visit, and it is almost a pleasure to wait for a table (no-reservation policy) when you are fed soft tender breads from the tandoori oven and soothing chai.

This dish is based on one of his recipes. It is so simple, you can't imagine it could be so good. Serve it with basmati rice.

Marinade

1 tsp (5 mL) grated lemon peel

1 tsp (5 mL) paprika
  (preferably smoked)

1 tsp (5 mL) salt

1 tsp (5 mL) ground cumin

2 tbsp (25 mL) vegetable oil

6 single boneless, skinless
  chicken breasts (about 2 lb/1 kg)

Topping

1/2 cup (125 mL) thinly sliced
  garlic

1/4 tsp (1 mL) cayenne

1/2 tsp (2 mL) salt

Pinch pepper

2 tbsp (25 mL) butter

1 tbsp (15 mL) vegetable oil

3/4 cup (175 mL) chopped
  roasted cashews

1 tbsp (15 mL) lemon juice

1. For marinade, in a small bowl, combine lemon peel, paprika, salt, cumin and oil. Rub into chicken and marinate for a few minutes or up to a few hours in refrigerator.

2. Meanwhile, for topping, in a small bowl, combine garlic, cayenne, salt and pepper.

3. Heat butter and oil in a small skillet on medium heat and add garlic. Cook until just golden, about 4 to 5 minutes. Do not let garlic brown too much or it will be bitter. Add cashews and lemon juice.

4. Grill chicken for about 5 minutes per side, or until just cooked through. Do not overcook.

5. Transfer chicken to serving plates and spoon garlic and cashew mixture on top.

Makes 6 servings

Green Thai Curry Chicken with Eggplant and Tofu

This is a sneaky way to get people to love tofu, as it is hard to tell what is tofu and what is chicken. Serve with steamed rice (page 126) or noodles.

Thai green and red curry pastes are available in supermarkets and Asian grocery stores. You can substitute pureed tomatoes or tomato sauce for part or all of the coconut milk.

3 tbsp (45 mL) vegetable oil,
    divided
1 lb (500 g) boneless skinless
    chicken breasts, cut in 1-inch
    (2.5 cm) cubes
8 oz (250 g) extra-firm tofu,
    cut in 1/2-inch (1 cm) cubes
1 Asian eggplant, cut in 1-inch
    (2.5 cm) cubes
1 onion, chopped
2 tbsp (25 mL) green Thai
    curry paste
1 cup (250 mL) coconut milk
1 tbsp (15 mL) Thai fish sauce
    or soy sauce
1/4 cup (50 mL) chopped fresh
    cilantro or basil

1. Heat 2 tbsp (25 mL) oil in a large, deep nonstick skillet or wok on medium-high heat. Add chicken and cook, stirring, for 3 to 4 minutes, or until brown. Remove chicken from pan. Add tofu to pan and cook for a few minutes, or until brown. Reserve with chicken. Add eggplant and cook for a few minutes, or until brown. Reserve with chicken.

2. Add remaining 1 tbsp (15 mL) oil to pan if necessary. Add onion. Cook for a few minutes. Add curry paste and cook for 30 to 60 seconds, or until fragrant. Add coconut milk and fish sauce. Bring to a boil.

3. Return chicken, tofu and eggplant to pan. Cook gently for 10 minutes. Sprinkle with cilantro.

Makes 4 to 6 servings

Thai Fish Sauce

This pungent, salty Asian flavoring is made with fermented fish or seafood (usually anchovies, crab or shrimp). If you don't like it or can't find it, use soy sauce instead. Store it in the refrigerator once it has been opened.

Roast Chicken

Roast chicken is a home-cooking classic. Everyone makes it a little bit differently, but as long as you buy a good-quality chicken and don't overcook it, it will taste great. Roasting it breast side down for the first twenty minutes keeps the breast meat juicy and tender. To turn the chicken easily, I use the new heatproof rubber gloves (True Blue). They are thicker than regular rubber gloves and are great for rubbing the skins off peppers, peeling hot beets or potatoes, or transferring a roast to a carving board. Just don't touch hot pans with them, or they will melt.

1 3 1/2-lb (2 kg) chicken

1 lemon

2 sprigs fresh rosemary

4 whole cloves garlic, peeled

1 tsp (5 mL) salt

1 onion, thickly sliced

1. Trim chicken and discard any fat from cavity. Pierce lemon in a few spots and place in cavity with rosemary and garlic. Truss chicken by tying legs together if you wish (but there will be more crispy skin if you don't). Tuck wings under neck. Sprinkle outside of chicken with salt.

2. Arrange onion slices in center of roasting pan and place chicken on top, breast side down.

3. Roast in a preheated 400 F (200 C) oven for 20 minutes. Turn chicken breast side up (if you don't have heatproof rubber gloves, use tea towels or regular oven mitts) and roast for 40 to 60 minutes longer, or until a meat thermometer inserted in thigh reads 165 F (72 C). Baste every 20 minutes during roasting. If chicken is browning too much, reduce heat to 350 F (180 C) and/or place a piece of foil over top.

4. Transfer chicken to a platter or carving board. Pour juices into a measuring cup. Add a few tablespoons of boiling water to roasting pan and scrape up any juices stuck to bottom. Add to juices in cup.

5. Cut chicken into serving pieces. Discard fat from juices and pour juices over chicken.

Makes 4 to 6 servings

Roast Turkey

My sister and I started cooking Thanksgiving dinner together when our kids were young and we all shared a cottage. At first I would simply buy a good-quality fresh turkey, stick it in the oven and call it a day. It was easy. Then Jani started to give me the gears (as only sisters can) about the fact that I was skipping the traditional trimmings that her friends always made. Although I am not usually very competitive, this really got me going, so I started to make gravy, cranberry sauce and stuffing (which I always make separately). And to be truthful, I have realized that for many people the trimmings are more important than the turkey itself.

The biggest secret to making a great turkey dinner is to buy a great turkey. Nothing compares with fresh, naturally raised or organic.

1 15-lb (7.5 kg) turkey

2 tbsp (25 mL) olive oil

2 tsp (10 mL) salt

1/2 tsp (2 mL) pepper

1 orange, quartered

1 lemon, quartered

1 onion, quartered

3 sprigs fresh rosemary

3 sprigs fresh sage

1 cup (250 mL) Port or water

Gravy

1/2 cup (125 mL) Port or water

2 cups (500 mL) turkey stock or
   chicken stock, approx.

3 tbsp (45 mL) butter or olive oil

1/4 cup (50 mL) all-purpose flour

1 tbsp (15 mL) soy sauce

1 tbsp (15 mL) lemon juice

1 tbsp (15 mL) Worcestershire
   sauce

1/2 tsp (2 mL) hot red
   pepper sauce

1. Remove neck and giblets from turkey and reserve for stock. Rub turkey inside and out with olive oil and sprinkle with salt and pepper. Fill cavity with orange, lemon, onion, rosemary and sage. Tie legs together to close cavity and truss if you wish.

2. Heat a lightly oiled roasting pan in a preheated 375 F (190 C) oven for 5 minutes. Add turkey, breast side down, and roast for 30 minutes. Gently turn turkey over (page 99). Add Port to roasting pan.

3. Reduce heat to 325 F (160 C) and continue to roast for 2 hours, or until a thermometer inserted into meaty part of thigh reads 165 F (72 C). Baste every 20 to 30 minutes.

4. When turkey is ready, remove to a serving platter or carving board. Remove fruit and vegetables from cavity and discard. Place a piece of foil over turkey and allow to rest while making gravy.

5. For gravy, pour any juices in roasting pan into a large measuring cup. Add Port or water to roasting pan. Place on medium-high heat and scrape bottom. Add to juices. Skim off and discard any fat from surface of juices. You should have about 1 cup (250 mL) liquid. Add enough turkey stock to make 3 cups (750 mL).

6. Heat butter in a large saucepan on medium-high heat. Add flour and cook for a few minutes until lightly browned. Add hot juices and bring to a boil. Add soy sauce, lemon juice, Worcestershire and hot pepper sauce. Cook for 5 minutes. Taste and adjust seasonings if necessary.

7. Carve turkey. Drizzle slices with gravy and pass remaining gravy at table.

Makes 8 to 10 servings

Mushroom Bread Stuffing

I like to bake stuffing separately rather than in the bird. It keeps the turkey meat juicier, because you only have to cook the turkey to 165 F (72 C). If the turkey is stuffed, it must be cooked longer so that the stuffing reaches 165 F (72 C), but by that time the meat is at 185 F (85 C). For added flavor, I drizzle the stuffing with the pan drippings before serving.

For a lower-fat version, use 2 tbsp (25 mL) olive oil to start the onions and drizzle the stuffing with turkey stock instead of the pan drippings.

1/3 cup (75 mL) butter or olive oil

2 onions, coarsely chopped

2 cloves garlic, finely chopped

3 stalks celery, sliced

2 leeks, trimmed and chopped

1 lb (500 g) mushrooms
(mixture of wild and cultivated),
trimmed and sliced

10 cups (2.5 L) crusty bread cubes
(about 1 lb/500 g)

2 cups (500 mL) turkey stock or
chicken stock

1/2 cup (125 mL) chopped
fresh parsley

1/4 cup (50 mL) chopped fresh
sage, or 1 tbsp (15 mL) dried

2 tbsp (25 mL) chopped
fresh thyme, or
1/2 tsp (2 mL) dried

1 tsp (5 mL) salt

1/2 tsp (2 mL) pepper

1. Melt butter in a large deep skillet or Dutch oven on medium-high heat. Add onions and garlic and cook for a few minutes until fragrant. Add celery and leeks. Cook for 5 minutes until softened.

2. Add mushrooms and cook for about 10 minutes, or until any liquid evaporates.

3. Add bread cubes, stock, parsley, sage, thyme, salt and pepper and combine well. Taste and adjust seasonings if necessary.

4. Place stuffing in an oiled 13- x 9-inch (3 L) baking dish. If you want the top crusty, leave uncovered. If you want it moist, cover with foil. Bake in a preheated 325 F (160 C) oven for 30 to 40 minutes, or until thoroughly heated. When turkey is cooked, spoon about 1/2 cup (125 mL) cooked turkey juices over stuffing.

Makes 8 to 10 servings

Cranberry Port Sauce

Making cranberry sauce is easy, and it is so much fun to watch it pop and thicken. Cranberries go especially well with orange and Port, but if you do not have Port, just use more orange juice. Serve this with turkey or as a spread on sandwiches.

In a large saucepan, combine 3 cups (750 mL) fresh or frozen cranberries, 1 cup (250 mL) brown sugar, 1/2 cup (125 mL) orange juice, 1/2 cup (125 mL) Port and 1 tbsp (15 mL) grated orange peel. Bring to a boil. Reduce heat and simmer for 5 to 10 minutes, or until cranberries pop and sauce thickens. Serve cold (sauce will gel when it cools).

Makes 2 cups (500 mL)

Grilled Beef Filets with Maple Chipotle Glaze

I always tell students that the most tender cuts of beef are from the part of the cow that is the farthest from the ground; the filet is the farthest. It is best cooked quickly and served rare to medium-rare. Because it is very expensive, use a meat thermometer so that you don't overcook it. You could also use a less expensive cut such as sirloin, flank or skirt steak.

This glaze also works well on salmon. Buy a 3-lb (1.5 kg) salmon fillet with bones and skin removed. Rub with glaze. Place on a parchment-lined baking sheet and roast in a preheated 425 F (220 C) oven for 20 to 25 minutes, or until just cooked through.

3 lb (1.5 kg) beef filet

Maple Chipotle Glaze
1/4 cup (50 mL) hoisin sauce
2 tbsp (25 mL) maple syrup
  or maple sugar
2 tbsp (25 mL) ketchup
2 tbsp (25 mL) soy sauce
1 tbsp (15 mL) pureed chipotles
1 tsp (5 mL) ground cumin
1 tsp (5 mL) roasted sesame oil

1. Trim filet of any visible fat or silverskin. Cut filet in half lengthwise. Cut each half into 4 pieces.

2. In a small bowl, combine hoisin sauce, maple syrup, ketchup, soy sauce, chipotles, cumin and sesame oil. Place filet and marinade in a large heavy-duty resealable plastic bag. Rub glaze into beef and marinate for 1 hour at room temperature or longer in refrigerator.

3. Grill meat for 2 minutes per side on high heat. Reduce heat to medium and continue to grill for about 4 to 5 minutes per side, or until a meat thermometer reaches 125 to 135 F (52 to 57 C) for medium-rare. Let rest for 5 minutes before serving. Serve steaks whole or cut in slices on the diagonal.

Makes 8 servings

Beef Short Ribs with Barbecue Sauce

Short ribs are a tough cut of meat, but when they are simmered slowly for a long time, they become meltingly tender and have amazing flavor. This version is pretty spicy, but you can always reduce the heat by omitting or reducing the chipotles. Serve it over mashed potatoes (page 116) or creamy polenta (page 127).

Lately I have seen restaurants serving short ribs in thick strips rather than chunks, which would also work well.

I like to use Bull's Eye Original barbecue sauce as a base for the sauce, but you could also use ketchup, tomato sauce or your favorite barbecue sauce.

12 3-inch (7.5 cm) chunks short ribs (about 6 lb/3 kg total)	1. Trim as much fat as possible from short ribs. In a small bowl, combine paprika, chili powder, brown sugar, cumin, dry mustard and salt. Rub into ribs. Marinate for 1 hour or up to overnight in refrigerator.

12 3-inch (7.5 cm) chunks
  short ribs (about 6 lb/3 kg total)

2 tbsp (25 mL) paprika
  (preferably smoked)

2 tbsp (25 mL) chili powder

2 tbsp (25 mL) brown sugar

1 tbsp (15 mL) ground cumin

1 tbsp (15 mL) dry mustard

2 tsp (10 mL) salt

Barbecue Sauce

2 tbsp (25 mL) vegetable oil

3 onions, chopped

8 cloves garlic, chopped

2 cups (500 mL) barbecue sauce

1 cup (250 mL) beer, red wine
  or water

1/4 cup (50 mL) soy sauce

1/4 cup (50 mL) brown sugar

1/4 cup (50 mL) Worcestershire
  sauce

2 tbsp (25 mL) balsamic vinegar or
  red wine vinegar

2 tbsp (25 mL) Dijon mustard

1 tbsp (15 mL) pureed chipotles

1. Trim as much fat as possible from short ribs. In a small bowl, combine paprika, chili powder, brown sugar, cumin, dry mustard and salt. Rub into ribs. Marinate for 1 hour or up to overnight in refrigerator.

2. Heat oil in a large Dutch oven or roasting pan on medium-high heat. Brown short ribs well on all sides (this will probably take at least 10 minutes). Remove from pan. Discard all but a few tablespoons of fat from pan.

3. Add onions and garlic to pan. Cook for 5 minutes, or until translucent and very fragrant. Add barbecue sauce, beer, soy sauce, brown sugar, Worcestershire sauce, vinegar, Dijon mustard and chipotles. Bring to a boil.

4. Place ribs in sauce. Cover top of ribs directly with a piece of parchment paper and then cover pan with lid or foil

5. Bake ribs in a preheated 350 F (180 C) oven for 2 1/2 to 3 hours, or until very tender. Check every hour to make sure there is enough liquid in pan. If necessary, add water.

6. Transfer ribs to a serving plate and keep warm. Skim any fat from sauce. Combine sauce with ribs and serve.

Makes 10 to 12 servings

Grilled Steak Espagnol

I could not believe that in this tiny fishing village in Spain, after course after course of fish, we were served this spectacular steak. It was sliced raw and then held together with long metal skewers. The salt and olive oil dripped down between the slices as it cooked, seasoning each piece. When the skewers were removed, the steak fell apart into serving-sized pieces.

2 1/2 lb (1.25 kg) sirloin steak,
   about 1 1/2 inches (4 cm) thick
2 tbsp (25 mL) olive oil
1 tbsp (15 mL) fleur de sel or
   Maldon salt, or 1 1/2 tbsp
   (22 mL) kosher salt

1. Rub steak generously with oil and salt on both sides.

2. Cut steak crosswise into 6 to 8 slices about 1 inch (2.5 cm) thick. Reassemble steak by running two long metal skewers through length in opposite directions.

3. Barbecue steak on high heat for 2 minutes per side. Reduce heat and cook for 4 to 5 minutes per side, or until a meat thermometer reaches 125 to 135 F (52 to 57 C) for medium-rare. Let rest for 5 minutes. Remove skewers and serve in slices.

Makes 6 to 8 servings

Korean-style Miami Ribs

Whenever I cook Miami ribs for a class, students rush home to make them. Miami ribs are thinly sliced short ribs. Generally short ribs are considered a tough cut that should be cooked for a long time, but when they are thinly sliced and marinated, they can be cooked quickly. Sometimes these are called Argentina ribs or crosscut short ribs, but whatever your butcher calls them, for barbecuing, ask for them to be sliced about 1/4 inch (5 mm) thick. Serve with steamed rice (page 126) and a cucumber and tomato salad.

1/2 cup (125 mL) soy sauce

1/3 cup (75 mL) granulated sugar

1 tbsp (15 mL) roasted sesame oil

3 cloves garlic, minced

2 lb (1 kg) Miami ribs (beef short
  ribs cut in 8 to 12 very thin strips)

2 tbsp (25 mL) toasted
  sesame seeds

3 green onions, thinly sliced
  on diagonal

1. In a small bowl, combine soy sauce, sugar, sesame oil and garlic.

2. Place Miami ribs in a shallow baking dish and pour on marinade. Cover and marinate at room temperature for 1 hour or up to overnight in refrigerator.

3. Remove ribs from marinade and pat dry. Place marinade in a small saucepan and cook until mixture thickens like a glaze.

4. Meanwhile, barbecue ribs for about 3 to 5 minutes per side, turning a few times and brushing with glaze each time. Sprinkle with sesame seeds and green onions before serving.

Makes 4 to 6 servings

Braised Herb Veal Breast with Gremolata

One of my mother's favorite dishes was old-fashioned veal breast. We had it all the time. So it was a big surprise to see it on the menus of some of the hottest New York restaurants. Their versions were definitely fancier than my mom's, but no one's was better.

This is especially good for entertaining because it is a perfect make-ahead dish. To fancy it up a bit, I've added gremolata (the traditional topping for osso bucco)—a vibrant blend of lemon peel, garlic and parsley. It is sprinkled over the dish at the end for the ultimate flavor boost, but you can omit it if you wish.

Serve this with mashed potatoes, creamy polenta or risotto.

1 4-lb (2 kg) veal breast, trimmed

1 tbsp (15 mL) salt

1 tsp (5 mL) pepper

1 tbsp (15 mL) chopped fresh
   rosemary, or 1/2 tsp (2 mL) dried

1 tbsp (15 mL) chopped fresh
   thyme, or 1/2 tsp (2 mL) dried

2 tbsp (25 mL) olive oil

5 large onions, chopped

10 cloves garlic, chopped

1 cup (250 mL) dry white wine

2 cups (500 mL) chicken stock
   or water

Gremolata

2 tbsp (25 mL) chopped fresh
   parsley

1 tbsp (15 mL) grated lemon peel

1 tbsp (15 mL) finely chopped
   garlic

1. Sprinkle veal on both sides with salt, pepper, rosemary and thyme. Roll up and tie securely.

2. Heat oil in a large Dutch oven or roasting pan on medium-high heat. Brown roast well on all sides (this should take 10 to 15 minutes). Remove from pan.

3. Add onions and garlic to pan. Cook for 2 minutes, or until wilted. Add wine and bring to a boil. Add stock and bring to a boil.

4. Place veal on onions. Place parchment paper directly on surface of meat. Cover pan with foil and then lid.

5. Cook in a preheated 325 F (160 C) oven for 4 hours, or until veal is very tender.

6. Meanwhile, to make gremolata, in a small bowl, combine parsley, lemon peel and garlic.

7. Remove veal from pan. Remove string. Cut into thick slices. Serve with juices and onions. (The juices can be pureed if you prefer.) Sprinkle with gremolata.

Makes 8 servings

Grilled Pork Chops with Braised Fennel and Rosemary

This is a recipe I developed for Maple Leaf Pork. The secret to preparing the new leaner style of pork is not to over-cook it. If the pork chops are on the bone, cook them for the longer cooking time.

To prepare the fennel, trim off the leaves and base. Cut the fennel bulb in half through the core. Cut each half into thin wedges so that a bit of the core keeps each piece intact. If you cannot find fennel, use a large sweet onion (e.g., Vidalia)—and, of course, change the name of the recipe.

4 pork chops, about 1 inch
  (2.5 cm) thick
2 tbsp (30 mL) olive oil, divided
1 clove garlic, finely chopped
1 tbsp (15 mL) chopped fresh
  rosemary, or 1/2 tsp (2 mL) dried
1 tsp (5 mL) salt
1/4 tsp (1 mL) pepper
1 large bulb fennel, trimmed and
  cut in thin wedges
  (about 1 lb/500 g)
1/3 cup (75 mL) balsamic vinegar
1/3 cup (75 mL) water
1 tbsp (15 mL) brown sugar
2 tbsp (25 mL) chopped
  fresh parsley

1. Pat pork chops dry and place in a shallow dish.

2. In a small bowl, combine 1 tbsp (15 mL) olive oil, garlic, rosemary, salt and pepper. Rub into pork chops. Marinate for at least 10 minutes, or up to overnight in refrigerator.

3. Heat remaining 1 tbsp (15 mL) oil in a large deep skillet on medium-high heat. Brown pork chops for 1 to 2 minutes per side, or until well browned. Remove from pan. Discard all but 1 tbsp (15 mL) fat from pan.

4. Add fennel wedges to pan. Cook for 1 to 2 minutes per side, or until light-ly browned. Add vinegar, water and sugar. Bring to a boil. Cook, uncovered, for 3 to 5 minutes, or until fennel is well colored and liquid is reduced by about half.

5. Return chops to pan with fennel and turn over in juices. Cover and cook on medium heat for 5 to 8 minutes, or until an instant-read meat thermome-ter reads 150 to 160 F (65 to 70 C).

6. Remove pork to a serving platter. Cook fennel, uncovered, for a few min-utes, or until juices are very syrupy. Spoon juices and fennel over pork. Sprinkle with parsley.

Makes 4 servings

Braised Lamb Shanks with Sweet Red Pepper Sauce

Although this dish contains tons of garlic, because the garlic is cooked so long, it tastes mild and sweet. Serve with mashed or scalloped potatoes, or over pasta, polenta or couscous. You can serve the lamb shanks whole or remove the meat from the bone before serving, so as not to scare guests with such a huge-looking hunk of meat (most of it is bone)! Removing the meat from the bones makes this a great buffet dish.

This recipe also works with short ribs.

8 lamb shanks, trimmed

1 cup (250 mL) dry red wine

1 tsp (5 mL) salt

1/4 tsp (1 mL) pepper

1 tbsp (15 mL) chopped fresh
  thyme, or 1/2 tsp (2 mL) dried

1 tbsp (15 mL) olive oil

3 onions, coarsely chopped

30 cloves garlic, peeled
  (about 3 heads)

1 jalapeño, seeded and chopped

1 tbsp (15 mL) ground cumin

4 sweet red peppers, peeled,
  cored and cut in 1-inch
  (2.5 cm) chunks

1 28-oz (796 mL) can plum
  tomatoes, with juices

1/4 cup (50 mL) coarsely
  chopped fresh parsley

1. Place lamb shanks in a large shallow dish. Pour wine over lamb and sprinkle with salt, pepper and thyme. Marinate overnight in refrigerator, turning lamb once or twice.

2. Heat oil in a heavy Dutch oven on medium-high heat. Pat lamb dry. Strain and reserve marinade. Brown lamb well on all sides, in batches if necessary. This should take about 15 minutes. Remove lamb from pan.

3. Add onions, garlic and jalapeño to pan and cook for a few minutes. Add cumin and cook for 2 minutes. Add red peppers. Reduce heat and cook gently for a few more minutes.

4. Add tomatoes and marinade to pan. Bring to a boil. Break up tomatoes with a spoon.

5. Return lamb shanks to pan. Cover and bake in a preheated 350 F (180 C) oven for 2 1/2 to 3 hours, or until very tender.

6. Remove lamb shanks from pan. Skim any fat from surface of sauce and discard. Puree sauce in a food processor or blender. Return sauce to pan. (If sauce is too thick, add water; if it is too thin, cook, uncovered, on medium-high heat until thickened.) Return lamb shanks to sauce and heat thoroughly.

7. Garnish lamb shanks with parsley.

Makes 8 servings

Baby Back Ribs with Chipotle Barbecue Sauce

When you prepare any kind of ribs, be sure to remove the membrane on the underside; the meat will be much more tender. Scrape a bit of the membrane away at one edge with a knife and then, using paper towels to help you, hold the ribs with one hand and rip the membrane away with the other. It may come off in a few pieces. Just do the best you can or ask the butcher to do this for you.

These ribs are pretty spicy. If you prefer less heat, reduce or omit the chipotles. For a dry version, bake the ribs in the sauce and rub the cooked ribs with the spice mixture before grilling.

2 tbsp (25 mL) paprika
 (preferably smoked)
2 tbsp (25 mL) brown sugar
2 tsp (10 mL) salt
2 tsp (10 mL) dry mustard
4 strips back ribs
 (about 5 lb/2.5 kg total)

Chipotle Barbecue Sauce
1 28-oz (796 mL) can plum
 tomatoes, drained and pureed
2 tbsp (25 mL) pureed chipotles
2 tbsp (25 mL) lemon juice
2 tbsp (25 mL) Worcestershire
 sauce
2 tbsp (25 mL) brown sugar
1 tbsp (15 mL) Dijon mustard

1. In a small bowl, combine paprika, sugar, salt and dry mustard.

2. Remove membrane on underside of ribs. Cut strips in two. Rub with spice mixture. Place in a shallow dish, cover and marinate for 1 hour at room temperature or up to overnight in refrigerator.

3. Place ribs on a foil-lined baking sheet (for easy cleanup). Cover with foil and cook in a preheated 300 F (150 C) oven for 1 1/2 hours.

4. Meanwhile, to make sauce, in a bowl, combine pureed tomatoes, chipotles, lemon juice, Worcestershire, brown sugar and Dijon mustard.

5. Drain ribs and brush with sauce. Barbecue for 5 to 8 minutes per side, basting with sauce, until hot and browned. (Alternatively, arrange ribs in a single layer on a foil-lined baking sheet, brush with sauce and roast, uncovered, at 400 F/200 C for 20 to 30 minutes.)

Makes 6 to 8 servings

Standing Rib Roast

Rib roast was a traditional Friday-night dinner at our house. It was always a big deal. My mom would bring it to the table and my dad would carve it and the juices would fly all over, the dog would bark, we would fight over the bones, and it was fun and delicious chaos!

To make carving easier, be sure to ask the butcher to cut off the chine bone. Let the roast rest for about 15 minutes after it comes out of the oven and cut the meat off the bones in one piece before slicing. (You can still fight over the bones.)

Although I never had Yorkshire pudding when I was a kid, I love to serve it with roast beef now.

1 standing rib roast of beef (3 ribs, about 6 lb/3 kg)	1. Trim meat and pat dry.

1 standing rib roast of beef
   (3 ribs, about 6 lb/3 kg)
2 tbsp (25 mL) olive oil
1 tbsp (15 mL) Dijon mustard
1 tbsp (15 mL) chopped fresh
   rosemary, or 1/2 tsp (2 mL) dried
2 cloves garlic, finely chopped
1 tsp (5 mL) pepper
1 tbsp (15 mL) kosher salt
1 cup (250 mL) fresh or bottled
   white horseradish, drained
   and rinsed

1. Trim meat and pat dry.
2. In a small bowl, combine olive oil, mustard, rosemary, garlic and pepper. Rub into meat. Allow to marinate for 1 hour at room temperature or a few hours in refrigerator.
3. Just before cooking, sprinkle entire roast with salt. Place roast in a roasting pan, bone side down. Roast in a preheated 450 F (230 C) oven for 30 minutes. Reduce heat to 375 F (190 C) and roast for 1 1/2 to 2 hours longer, or until meat reaches 135 F (57 C) on a meat thermometer for medium-rare.
4. Transfer meat to a carving board and let rest for 15 minutes before carving. To carve, cut away bones. Position meat on carving board as if bones were still there (i.e., bone side down). Carve meat into slices against the grain. Cut bones into individual ribs and offer them to guests (or auction to the highest bidder; they are the best!).
5. Serve with horseradish

Makes 10 servings

Yorkshire Pudding

The first time I made this for my children, they were shocked that you could have a pudding that wasn't sweet. Even when I explained that in England, some puddings are savory and some are sweet, they were still skeptical.

Whisk 3 eggs in a large bowl.

Whisk in 1 cup (250 mL) milk until frothy. Quickly beat in 1 cup (250 mL) all-purpose flour and 1 tsp (5 mL) salt. Refrigerate for 30 minutes.

Divide 3 tbsp (45 mL) beef fat from roast beef (or use vegetable oil) among 12 nonstick muffin pans. Place in a preheated 450 F (230 C) oven for 5 minutes.

Spoon batter into hot pan (fat should sizzle). Bake for 10 minutes (do not open oven door during cooking time). Reduce oven temperature to 350 F (180 C) and bake for 10 minutes longer. Serve immediately.

Makes 12 puddings

Side Dishes

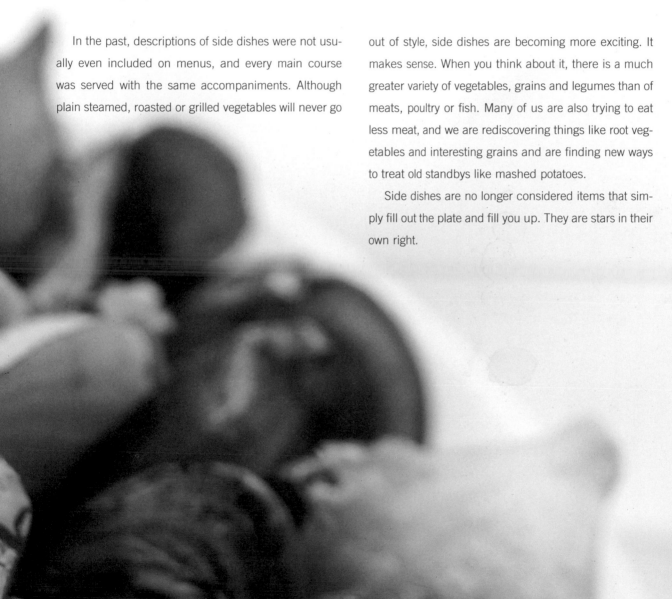

I recognized how important side dishes had become when I led a cooking tour in San Francisco and realized we were all choosing our main course on the basis of its side dishes. Each main course came with different sides, and they were all listed in mouth-watering detail on the menu.

In the past, descriptions of side dishes were not usually even included on menus, and every main course was served with the same accompaniments. Although plain steamed, roasted or grilled vegetables will never go out of style, side dishes are becoming more exciting. It makes sense. When you think about it, there is a much greater variety of vegetables, grains and legumes than of meats, poultry or fish. Many of us are also trying to eat less meat, and we are rediscovering things like root vegetables and interesting grains and are finding new ways to treat old standbys like mashed potatoes.

Side dishes are no longer considered items that simply fill out the plate and fill you up. They are stars in their own right.

Roasted Root Vegetables with Maple Balsamic Dressing

I am a very reluctant driver, so I was hesitant when PR diva Danielle Iversen asked me to participate in a National Ovarian Cancer Association fundraiser that involved "exploring the limits of vehicle control." The other participants and winners from Holt Renfrew Girls' Night In were thrilled to be included in the first level BMW Advanced Driver Training Course. And in the end, so was I. Not only did I learn a lot and gain driving confidence that day, but I picked up a recipe as well. This is an adaptation of a dish from En Ville Catering chef Rene Kramer, who catered the amazing lunch.

You can use many kinds of vegetables, including parsnips, potatoes, celeriac, red onions and beets, but I recently started making this with a combination of orange and yellow vegetables—an idea inspired by Vicki Westgate, a Kingston jewelry designer.

2 lb (1 kg) sweet potatoes (about 4), peeled and cut in rounds 1/2 inch (1 cm) thick

2 lb (1 kg) carrots, peeled and cut in 1/2-inch (1 cm) slices on the diagonal

1 lb (500 g) squash, peeled and cut in 2-inch (5 cm) wedges

2 sweet orange peppers, seeded and cut in thick strips

2 tbsp (25 mL) vegetable oil

Maple Balsamic Dressing

2 tbsp (25 mL) balsamic vinegar

2 tbsp (25 mL) red wine vinegar

2 tbsp (25 mL) brown sugar

2 tbsp (25 mL) maple syrup

2 tbsp (25 mL) chopped fresh thyme, or 1/2 tsp (2 mL) dried

1/2 tsp (2 mL) salt

1/4 tsp (1 mL) pepper

2 tbsp (25 mL) chopped fresh parsley

1. In a large bowl, combine sweet potatoes, carrots, squash and peppers. Toss with oil. Spread vegetables on one or two large parchment-lined baking sheets. Roast in a preheated 375 F (190 C) oven for 45 to 60 minutes, or until browned. Stir once or twice during cooking.

2. To prepare dressing, in a small bowl, combine vinegars, sugar, maple syrup, thyme, salt and pepper.

3. Toss hot roasted vegetables with dressing. Sprinkle with parsley.

Makes 8 servings

Stuffed Baked Potatoes with Herb Cheese

These potatoes are very versatile. They can be served as a vegetarian main course or as an especially delicious side dish with steak. The filling is also great served as mashed potatoes. You can make them ahead and reheat just before serving.

3 large baking potatoes
   (about 12 oz/375 g each)
1 cup (250 mL) crumbled
   herb cream cheese
   (about 6 oz/175 g)
1 green onion, chopped
1 tbsp (15 mL) chopped
   fresh tarragon, or 1/2 tsp
   (2 mL) dried
1 tsp (5 mL) salt
1/2 tsp (2 mL) pepper
1/4 cup (50 mL) milk, hot, optional

1. Scrub potatoes. Pierce with a fork in a few places. Place on a baking sheet and bake in a preheated 400 F (200 C) oven for 1 to 1 1/2 hours, or until potatoes are very tender.

2. Cut potatoes in half lengthwise and gently scoop out potato, leaving shells intact.

3. In a bowl, mash potato with cheese, green onion, tarragon, salt and pepper until smooth. If mixture is very thick, add a little hot milk. Spoon or pipe mashed potatoes back into potato shells.

4. Arrange potatoes on a baking sheet. Just before serving, reheat at 400 F (200 C) for 30 minutes, or until thoroughly heated and lightly browned.

Makes 6 servings

I love potatoes—

I would take them with me to a desert island. And mashed potatoes are high on my list of ways to prepare them. Kids and adults love them, and they are very versatile. I even make a mashed potato salad (page 53).

In the past few years, many restaurants have returned to comfort foods, and several menus now feature mashed potatoes with flavorful ingredients added, from roasted garlic to wild mushrooms, lobster and foie gras.

Mashed Potato Tips

• For lower-fat mashed potatoes, replace the butter with one-third the amount of olive oil. Use low-fat milk or potato-cooking water instead of cream.

• For mashed potatoes, use baking potatoes (e.g., russets or Idaho) or Yukon Golds.

• For really creamy mashed potatoes, always heat the liquid before adding.

• For a silky-smooth texture, put the potatoes through a potato ricer or food mill to mash them. No chance of lumps. (Do not mash potatoes in a food processor; they will turn out like glue.)

• For chunkier mashed potatoes, just mash with a potato masher. You can even use large red-skinned potatoes and leave the skins on.

• For truly luxurious mashed potatoes, add a spoonful or two of white truffle oil (available in fancy food shops).

Roasted Garlic

I use lots of roasted garlic. Sometimes people are nervous about using so much garlic, but after it is roasted it is soft, sweet and luscious. (One whole head of roasted garlic is less potent than one clove of raw garlic.)

Roasted garlic adds richness to soups and pasta sauces; it makes mashed potatoes, salad dressings and dips creamy and thick. Sometimes I blend it with goat cheese and herbs and use it as a spread on toasted bread. Don't be without it. You can roast lots and keep it in the refrigerator for a week or two, or you can squeeze out the garlic, freeze it in small heavy-duty resealable plastic bags and break off what you need.

To roast garlic, remove any excess white papery skin from 4 whole heads of garlic. Cut top quarter from each head (the pointed part) so that the tops of the cloves are exposed. Rub cut surfaces with a little olive oil.

Wrap garlic heads in foil in a single layer and roast at 375 F (190 C) for 40 to 50 minutes, or until garlic is very tender when squeezed

Cool heads slightly and squeeze out garlic. (It is easier to squeeze when still warm.)

You can also peel many cloves of raw garlic—make lots—drizzle with olive oil and roast in a baking dish at 350 F (180 C) for 40 to 50 minutes, or until tender and fragrant. Drain off the oil and use as garlic oil for cooking (keep it refrigerated; it will solidify but melt again at room temperature).

Roasted Garlic Mayonnaise

In a food processor or bowl, combine 2 heads roasted garlic with 1/2 cup (125 mL) mayonnaise. Process or mash until smooth. Add 2 tsp (10 mL) lemon juice and dash hot red pepper sauce and combine.

Makes about 1/2 cup (125 mL)

Mashed Potatoes with Bacon and Mushrooms

In this dish, just a small amount of bacon seasons the potatoes really well, but of course you could always use more. Use double-smoked bacon if you can find it.

3 lb (1.5 kg) Yukon Gold or baking potatoes (about 6 large), peeled and cut in chunks

2 slices bacon, diced

4 cloves garlic, finely chopped

8 oz (250 g) cremini mushrooms, coarsely chopped

1 cup (250 mL) milk or cream

2 tbsp (25 mL) chopped fresh parsley

3 tbsp (45 mL) butter

2 tsp (10 mL) salt

1. Cook potatoes in a large pot of boiling salted water. Reduce heat and cook gently for 20 to 25 minutes, or until potatoes are very tender.

2. Meanwhile, in a large skillet, cook bacon on medium-high heat for a few minutes, or until crisp. Remove bacon and reserve. Remove all but about 1 tbsp (15 mL) fat from pan.

3. Add garlic to skillet. Cook, stirring, for a minute until fragrant, but do not brown. Add mushrooms and cook until any liquid in pan has evaporated and mushrooms have browned. Add milk and parsley and cook for a few minutes to heat milk.

4. Drain potatoes well. Return to pot and mash coarsely. Add butter and salt. Beat in mushroom mixture and reserved bacon. Add more hot milk if potatoes are too thick. Taste and adjust seasonings if necessary.

Makes 8 servings

Mashed Potatoes with Corn and Garlic

While potatoes are cooking, melt 3 tbsp (45 mL) butter in a medium skillet on low heat. Add 3 finely chopped garlic cloves and 1/2 tsp (2 mL) ground cumin and cook for a few minutes until fragrant. Add 2 cups (500 mL) fresh or frozen corn kernels. Increase heat to medium and cook for 2 minutes. Add 2 thinly sliced green onions, 3/4 cup (175 mL) milk or cream, 2 tsp (10 mL) salt and 1/4 tsp (1 mL) pepper and heat.

Drain potatoes well and mash. Stir in corn mixture. Add extra hot milk or cream if potatoes are too thick. Taste and adjust seasonings if necessary.

Makes 6 to 8 servings

Roasted Garlic Mashed Potatoes

Drain potatoes, reserving about 1 cup (250 mL) cooking liquid. Squeeze garlic from 4 heads roasted garlic into potatoes and mash. Add 1/4 cup (50 mL) olive oil or butter and enough potato-cooking liquid (or hot milk or cream) to create a creamy consistency. Add salt and pepper to taste.

Sprinkle potatoes with chopped fresh chives and 1 tbsp (15 mL) truffle oil, if desired.

Makes 6 to 8 servings

Double Potato Gratin

This wonderful version of scalloped potatoes comes from Olga Truchan, the food stylist who is responsible for the beautiful food in the photographs in my books. Potato gratins are often loaded with cream, butter and cheese, but this version is much lighter and is every bit as delicious. It has amazing flavor and, of course, looks absolutely stunning.

3 lb (1.5 kg) Yukon Gold or
   baking potatoes (about 6 large)
1 lb (500 g) sweet potatoes
   (about 2)
1 tbsp (15 mL) butter, divided
1/4 cup (50 mL) olive oil, approx.
2 tsp (10 mL) salt
1 tsp (5 mL) pepper
1 tbsp (15 mL) chopped fresh
   rosemary or thyme,
     or 1/2 tsp (2 mL) dried

1. Peel potatoes and sweet potatoes and cut into slices 1/4 inch (5 mm) thick.

2. Place a piece of parchment paper in bottom of a 9-inch (2 L) baking dish and butter with half the butter. Arrange a layer of regular potatoes over bottom of dish. Sprinkle potatoes with a little olive oil, salt, pepper and rosemary. Continue to layer and sprinkle potatoes until you have used half the potatoes.

3. Arrange sweet potato slices on top, sprinkling with oil, salt, pepper and rosemary after each layer.

4. Continue to arrange remaining potatoes in layers on top of sweet potatoes, sprinkling after each layer.

5. Butter another piece of parchment paper with remaining butter. Place paper, butter side down, on top of potatoes. Weigh down paper with a heavy ovenproof dish or foil-covered bricks.

6. Bake in a preheated 425 F (220 C) oven for 1 hour, or until potatoes are tender. Remove weights and paper. Let potatoes sit for 5 minutes.

7. Invert dish onto a serving platter and remove remaining piece of parchment paper. Serve with the best-looking side up.

Makes 6 to 8 servings

Potato Pancakes (Latkes)

Potato pancakes are served at Hanukkah, and they are one of the most delicious of all Jewish foods. I like to dedicate a whole meal to them and eat them hot out of the pan. But many people serve latkes as a side dish with roasts. I like them with sour cream or yogurt, but others prefer applesauce.

For a lower-fat version, spray a nonstick baking sheet with cooking spray, drop batter onto prepared pan, flatten and bake at 450 F (230 C) for 10 to 15 minutes, or until browned and crisp on the bottom. Flip pancakes and cook second side for 5 to 10 minutes.

1 onion, cut in chunks

2 eggs

3 large baking potatoes,
   peeled and cut in chunks
   (about 1 1/2 lb/750 g total)

1 tsp (5 mL) salt

1/4 tsp (1 mL) pepper

3 tbsp (45 mL) cornflake crumbs
   or matzo meal

1/2 cup (125 mL) vegetable oil,
   approx.

1. In a food processor, chop onion finely. Add eggs and blend. Add potato chunks and process on/off until potatoes are chopped into egg mixture and there are no large chunks of potatoes left. (Do not overchop.) Mix in salt, pepper and cornflake crumbs.

2. Heat about 1/4 inch (5 mm) oil in a large nonstick skillet on medium-high heat. Add batter by tablespoonful, flattening latkes with back of a spoon. Cook for 2 to 3 minutes, or until browned and crisp. Turn and cook second side. Drain on paper towels. Repeat with remaining batter, adding oil between batches as necessary.

Makes about 16 pancakes

Roasted Plum Tomatoes

You can never have too many roasted plum tomatoes. They have an intense tomato flavor because their liquid evaporates as they cook. They can be served as a side dish or added pureed (or not) to a pasta sauce or soup. They can be chopped and added to risotto during the last few minutes of cooking; they are also great on pizza. They should keep in the refrigerator for up to a week, or you can freeze them.

3 lb (1.5 kg) plum tomatoes
  (12 to 15)
2 tbsp (25 mL) olive oil
1 tsp (5 mL) salt
1/2 tsp (2 mL) pepper
1 tbsp (15 mL) chopped fresh
  rosemary, or 1/2 tsp (2 mL) dried
1 tbsp (15 mL) chopped fresh
  thyme, or 1/2 tsp (2 mL) dried

1. Remove cores from tomatoes. Cut tomatoes in half crosswise and gently squeeze out excess seeds. Place cut side up on a parchment-lined baking sheet (cut a tiny slice off bottoms if necessary so they will sit upright).

2. Drizzle or spray tomatoes with olive oil and sprinkle with salt, pepper, rosemary and thyme. Roast in a preheated 400 F (200 C) oven for 45 to 50 minutes, or until some juices have evaporated and tomatoes are starting to brown on the bottom. Arrange tomatoes attractively on a serving plate. Serve warm or cold.

Makes 24 to 30

Succotash

Succotash makes a wonderful side dish for grilled chicken, chops or steak. I love using edamame (fresh soy beans) instead of the traditional lima beans. You can add squash, fennel, peppers or anything that tastes like fall. If you wish, omit the bacon and use 2 tbsp (25 mL) olive oil to cook the vegetables.

2 strips bacon, diced

1 small onion, chopped

2 cups (500 mL) fresh or
  frozen lima beans or edamame
  (fresh soy beans)

2 cups (500 mL) fresh or
  frozen corn kernels

1 tsp (5 mL) salt

1/4 tsp (1 mL) pepper

2 tbsp (25 mL) chopped
  fresh tarragon,
  or 1/2 tsp (2 mL) dried

1. In a large skillet on medium-high heat, cook bacon for a few minutes, or until crisp. Remove bacon and reserve. Discard all but 1 tbsp (15 mL) fat from skillet.

2. Add onion to skillet and cook for 2 minutes. Add beans and cook, stirring, for 5 minutes.

3. Add corn and combine well. Cook gently for 5 minutes longer. Add salt, pepper, tarragon and bacon. Taste and adjust seasonings if necessary.

Makes 4 to 6 servings

Grilled Vegetable Platter with Basil Balsamic Vinaigrette

A platter of grilled veggies is a great addition to almost any menu. It looks generous and colorful and is a celebration of plenty. You can add chunks of grilled corn, cherry tomatoes or any colorful steamed vegetable. Garnish the platter with sprigs of fresh basil.

Grilled vegetables also make a wonderful topping for a vegetarian pizza or pasta, or they can be pureed with chicken stock to make a flavorful soup.

Cut the fennel in wedges through the core, so it does not fall apart on the grill.

1 bulb fennel, trimmed and
  cut in wedges
2 medium zucchini, cut in 1/2-inch
  (1 cm) slices on the diagonal
2 Asian eggplants, cut in 1/2-inch
  (1 cm) slices on the diagonal
1 large sweet onion, peeled and
  sliced in 1/2-inch (1 cm) rounds
2 portobello mushrooms, trimmed
  and cut in thick slices
1 lb (500 g) asparagus, trimmed
2 tbsp (25 mL) olive oil
1 tsp (5 mL) salt
2 sweet red peppers (or 1 red and
  1 yellow), halved, cored
  and seeded

Basil Balsamic Vinaigrette
1 clove garlic, minced
1 tsp (5 mL) salt
2 tbsp (25 mL) balsamic vinegar
1/4 cup (50 mL) olive oil
2 tbsp (25 mL) chopped fresh basil

1. Drizzle fennel, zucchini, eggplants, onion, mushrooms and asparagus with olive oil and sprinkle with salt. Grill for a few minutes per side until browned and cooked through. Arrange each vegetable in rows on a large serving platter.

2. Grill peppers, skin side down, for a few minutes, or until blackened. Cool and peel. Cut into strips and arrange on platter with other vegetables.

3. For dressing, in a small bowl, combine garlic, salt and vinegar. Whisk in oil. Add basil. Taste and adjust seasonings if necessary.

4. Drizzle dressing over vegetables.

Makes 6 servings

Edamame and Green Bean Stir-fry

If you are unfamiliar with fresh (or frozen) soy beans (edamame), they are a wonderful surprise. You can buy them at Asian markets but they are also available in many supermarkets now. They are sold either in the pod or shelled. If you can only find them in the pod, just boil them in salted water for about 5 minutes and then squeeze them out of the shells.

If you cannot find edamame, use baby lima beans or peas or more green beans (buy the thin French green beans if you can find them).

2 tsp (10 mL) vegetable oil

1 clove garlic, finely chopped

1 lb (500 g) green beans,
  trimmed and cut in half
  on the diagonal

8 oz (250 g) sugar snap peas or
  snow peas, trimmed

1 lb (500 g) shelled edamame
  (about 3 cups/750 mL)

1/4 cup (50 mL) water

1/2 tsp (2 mL) salt

1 tbsp (15 mL) grated lemon peel

1 tbsp (15 mL) chopped fresh mint

1. Heat oil in a wok or large skillet on medium-high heat. Add garlic and cook, stirring, for 10 seconds, or until fragrant. Do not brown.

2. Add green beans and sugar snaps and stir-fry for 30 seconds. Add edamame and stir-fry for 30 seconds.

3. Add water and salt. Bring to a boil and cook for 3 to 4 minutes, or until vegetables are bright green and tender. Most of water should have evaporated.

4. Add lemon peel and mint and toss. Taste and adjust seasonings if necessary.

Makes 4 to 6 servings

Biryani Rice Pilaf

This is a delicious quick pilaf with exotic flavors. Traditional Indian recipes usually call for ghee—browned clarified butter that you can buy at Indian food shops or make yourself.

2 cups (500 mL) basmati rice

2 tbsp (25 mL) ghee or
  vegetable oil

1 onion, chopped

2 tbsp (25 mL) curry paste

1/4 cup (50 mL) tomato sauce

2 1/2 cups (625 mL) water

1 tsp (5 mL) salt

1 tsp (5 mL) lemon juice

2 tbsp (25 mL) chopped fresh
  cilantro

1. Rinse rice well and soak in cold water for 30 minutes. Drain well.

2. Heat ghee in a large saucepan on medium-high heat. Add onion and cook for 5 to 7 minutes, or until tender and slightly browned.

3. Add curry paste and cook for a few minutes. Add rice and cook, stirring, for a few minutes longer. Add tomato sauce and cook, stirring, for another few minutes.

4. Add water and bring to a boil. Cover, reduce heat and simmer for about 20 minutes, or until rice is tender and water has been absorbed.

5. Add salt and lemon juice. Taste and adjust seasonings if necessary. Sprinkle with cilantro.

Makes 6 servings

Steamed Rice

Kids and adults all love rice. There are as many ways to cook it as there are varieties and countries that have it as their staple, but plain steamed rice is an essential.

Rinse 2 cups (500 mL) basmati rice well in several changes of water. If you have time, place rice in a bowl and cover with 6 cups (1.5 L) cold water for 30 minutes (this shortens the cooking time slightly and keeps the grains very white). Drain well.

Place rice in a medium saucepan. Add 2 1/2 cups (625 mL) cold water. Bring to a boil, uncovered. Reduce heat to medium and cook for 5 to 7 minutes, or until water is absorbed and potholes appear on surface.

Cover rice. Reduce heat to low and cook for 10 minutes. Turn off heat but leave rice covered for 10 minutes longer. Fluff gently before serving.

Makes 4 servings

Grilled Polenta

Polenta can be served in many different ways. I often serve it under Cornish hens, grilled liver, steak or lamb chops. I also love it served as a first course topped with a sauce or a sauté of wild mushrooms. You can add an extra cup of liquid and serve it freshly made and creamy, but many people prefer a firm version like this one, as the texture is more familiar. After the polenta firms up, you can broil it, roast it, fry it or just reheat it in the pan at 400 F (200 C) for 20 to 30 minutes, but for the most delicious results, I like to grill it.

I use quick-cooking cornmeal for polenta as it cooks so quickly and tastes pretty good. If you use regular cornmeal, cook the polenta slowly, stirring often, until tender—about 30 minutes.

10 cups (2.5 L) milk or water, or
  a combination
1 tbsp (15 mL) salt
1/2 tsp (2 mL) pepper
2 cups (500 mL) quick-cooking
  cornmeal
1 tbsp (15 mL) white truffle oil,
  optional
2 tbsp (25 mL) olive oil

1. Place milk or water in a large deep saucepan and bring to a boil. Add salt and pepper.

2. Whisk in cornmeal slowly. Cook, stirring constantly, for 5 minutes. Stir in truffle oil if using. Taste and adjust seasonings if necessary.

3. Pour polenta into a 13- x 9-inch (3 L) parchment-lined baking dish. Cool and refrigerate until ready to cook. (Polenta can be made ahead to this point.)

4. Brush polenta with olive oil and cut into squares. Grill on a barbecue or grill pan for a couple of minutes on each side, or until browned and crisp.

Makes 8 to 12 servings

Grilled Corn on the Cob

I like to grill corn directly on the barbecue. It only takes a few minutes, and barbecuing gives the corn a smoky, earthy flavor. Serve it on the cob as a side dish or cut the kernels off the cob to add to salads, soups and breads.

This is at its best at the height of corn season, and the faster you get corn to the pot or grill the better, as the natural sugars quickly turn into starch after picking.

6 ears corn

2 tbsp (25 mL) olive oil or
  soft butter

1/2 tsp (2 mL) salt

2 tbsp (25 mL) chopped fresh basil

1. Remove husks and silk from corn. Place on a medium-high barbecue and keep turning corn until lightly browned on all sides. This usually takes 3 to 4 minutes.

2. In a small bowl, combine oil, salt and basil. Brush lightly on hot corn.

Makes 6 servings

Asparagus Risotto

Risotto is cooked in a way that results in a luxurious, creamy mass, but each grain of rice remains distinct. The texture is achieved by stirring the rice as it cooks so that the grains constantly rub against each other to create that creaminess.

Risotto should be cooked just before serving, but you can prepare it ahead up to the point of adding the rice. Many people say the proper way to serve risotto is *al dente*, but I prefer it cooked a minute or two longer. Be careful, however, as it is very easy to overcook it.

1 lb (500 g) asparagus, trimmed

6 cups (1.5 L) chicken stock or
  vegetable stock, approx.

2 tbsp (25 mL) olive oil

1 onion, chopped

1 carrot, diced

2 cups (500 mL) uncooked
  short-grain Italian rice

2 tbsp (25 mL) butter

1/2 cup (125 mL) grated
  Parmesan cheese

1 tsp (5 mL) salt

1/2 tsp (2 mL) pepper

1. Bring a skillet of water to a boil. Add asparagus and cook for 3 minutes. Drain and rinse with cold water to stop cooking. Reserve a few cooked asparagus tips for a garnish and dice the rest.

2. Meanwhile, bring stock to a boil in a saucepan.

3. Heat oil in a large saucepan on medium heat. Add onion and carrot and cook gently until tender but not brown, about 5 minutes. Add rice and stir to coat well with oil. Cook for 2 minutes.

4. Add about 1 cup (250 mL) boiling stock. Cook, stirring, until all liquid is absorbed. Continue to add liquid about 1/2 cup (125 mL) at a time, stirring almost continually, and cooking until all liquid is absorbed before each addition of stock. After about 10 minutes, stir in asparagus. Continue to add liquid until rice is tender, about 5 minutes longer. (Once you start to add liquid, it should take 17 to 20 minutes to cook rice. If the rice is not yet tender but you have run out of stock, simply use boiling water.)

5. Stir in butter, cheese, salt and pepper. Taste and adjust seasonings if necessary. Serve immediately.

Makes 8 servings

Corn Risotto with Chipotles and Cilantro

This unusual risotto combines an Italian technique with Southwestern flavors. There are three relatively easy-to-find types of Italian short-grain rice suitable for making risotto. I like Vialone Nano the best because it stays firm even a few minutes after it is cooked, but Arborio and Carnaroli are also good.

6 cups (1.5 L) vegetable stock
  or chicken stock

2 tbsp (25 mL) olive oil

3 cloves garlic, finely chopped

1 onion, finely chopped

2 tsp (10 mL) pureed chipotles,
  or 1 jalapeño, seeded and
  chopped

2 cups (500 mL) uncooked
  short-grain Italian rice

2 cups (500 mL) fresh or frozen
  corn kernels

2 tbsp (25 mL) butter

1 tsp (5 mL) salt

1/2 tsp (2 mL) pepper

1/2 cup (125 mL) coarsely
  chopped fresh cilantro

2 tbsp (25 mL) toasted pine nuts

1 cup (250 mL) grated smoked
  mozzarella cheese

1. In a saucepan, bring stock to a boil.

2. Meanwhile, heat oil in a large deep skillet or Dutch oven on medium-high heat. Add garlic and onion and cook, stirring, for a few minutes, or until fragrant but not brown. Add chipotles and cook for about 30 seconds. Stir in rice and cook, stirring, for about 2 minutes.

3. Start adding stock about 1/2 cup (125 mL) at a time, stirring constantly, until liquid has evaporated. After half of liquid has been added, add corn and stir well. Continue adding stock until all is used. If rice is not yet tender, add boiling water. This should take 17 to 20 minutes.

4. When rice is tender, add butter, salt and pepper. Sprinkle with cilantro, pine nuts and cheese. Taste and adjust seasonings if necessary. Stir gently just before serving.

Makes 6 servings

Leftovers

Leftovers I love leftovers. And, like most people, I can't resist standing in front of the open fridge and nibbling out of all the little containers. Some dishes, such as braised lamb shanks and short ribs, even taste better made ahead and warmed up the next day. However, most things are never quite the same when you try to serve them in their original form a second time. A roast turkey is only a roast turkey once.

The trick is to turn the leftovers into something completely different and, as Jacques Pépin once said when he was teaching here, you should never actually call them leftovers.

Cut up yesterday's steak and toss with vegetables and a mustard vinaigrette to make a steak salad. Use leftover roasted vegetables to make a vegetable soup, or use as a pizza topping.

Risotto is one dish that doesn't recycle well when it is just reheated. But you can turn it into delicious risotto cakes—crunchy on the outside and creamy on the inside. They are so good that it is worth making risotto just for this purpose.

Risotto Cakes

Combine 3 to 4 cups (750 mL to 1 L) cooked risotto with 1 beaten egg. Shape into patties about 3 inches (7.5 cm) in diameter and 3/4 inch (2 cm) thick.

Heat 2 tbsp (25 mL) butter and 2 tbsp (25 mL) olive oil in a large skillet on medium-high heat. Add risotto cakes and cook for about 5 minutes per side, or until browned and crusty. Serve plain or with tomato sauce.

Makes 3 to 4 patties

Day Breakfasts

There are meat and potato people, and then there are breakfast people. I could eat breakfast at any time. When I was growing up, we would often have pan- cakes or an omelette for dinner, and that still suits me fine.

Breakfast and brunch have also become popular meals for entertaining. The pace is leisurely, the atmos- phere is casual and you don't have to stay up past your bedtime. Brunch dishes are also simpler and less expen- sive than most main courses, and you don't have to serve alcohol. And, once you've eaten a late, hearty breakfast, you hardly need to eat for the rest of the day!

Cheese Blintzes with Marinated Strawberries
My mother made incredible blintzes. Some people make blintzes with cream cheese, but my mom made hers with cottage cheese, which is not as rich (you can also use a combination). Be sure to buy the right kind of cottage cheese. It must be the solid-curd or pressed cottage cheese, not the looser kind sold in tubs.

At a party I went to recently, the blintzes were made by Toronto caterer Mary Marlow. She did not fry them the way my mother did, but instead folded them up loosely, placed them seam side down in a baking dish and baked them in the oven. Now I usually do the same thing. It's easier, and you use less butter.

Serve these with marinated strawberries or Spiced Berry Compote, with or without sour cream.

Blintzes
6 eggs
1 1/2 cups (375 mL) milk
1 tbsp (15 mL) granulated sugar
Pinch salt
1 1/2 cups (375 mL)
 all-purpose flour
2 tbsp (25 mL) butter

Filling
1 1/2 lb (750 g) solid-curd
 cottage cheese
3 tbsp (45 mL) granulated sugar
2 eggs
Pinch salt

Marinated Strawberries
4 cups (1 L) fresh strawberries
2 tbsp (25 mL) granulated sugar
1 tbsp (15 mL) lemon juice or
 balsamic vinegar

1. To make batter for blintzes, combine eggs, milk, sugar, salt and flour in a food processor or bowl. Let rest, covered, for about 30 minutes.

2. Melt butter in an 8- or 9-inch (20 cm or 23 cm) nonstick skillet on medium-high heat. Whisk melted butter into batter.

3. Return skillet to heat and add about 1/2 cup (125 mL) batter. Swirl batter around skillet and pour excess back into bowl so blintz will be very thin. Cook until brown, about 1 to 2 minutes. Flip out onto a clean tea towel. Repeat until all batter is used. Stack blintzes on top of each other in four piles.

4. For filling, in a large bowl, blend together cottage cheese, sugar, eggs and salt.

5. Place crêpes cooked side down on work surface. Place about 3 tbsp (45 mL) filling in middle of each. Loosely fold in sides. Place crêpes overlapping in a lightly buttered 13- x 9-inch (3 L) baking dish, folded side down.

6. Bake in a preheated 375 F (190 C) oven for 20 minutes, or until hot.

7. Meanwhile, in a bowl, combine strawberries, sugar and lemon juice. Marinate at room temperature for at least 15 minutes. Serve with blintzes.

Makes 16 blintzes

Spiced Berry Compote
Serve this sauce with pancakes, blintzes or desserts such as lemon tart (page 174) or cheesecake (page 184).

Sprinkle 1/2 cup (125 mL) granulated sugar over bottom of a large deep skillet. Cook on medium-high heat, without stirring, until sugar melts and browns.

Add 1/2 cup (125 mL) red wine and 1 cinnamon stick. Mixture will bubble up. Cook for a few minutes.

Add 3 cups (750 mL) mixed fresh berries. Bring to a boil. Remove from heat. (Do not overcook fruit.) Serve warm or cold.

Makes about 3 cups (750 mL)

Lemon Blueberry Scones

Scones are as popular now as muffins were a few years ago. The ones you buy at coffee shops, though, are usually not very moist or tender. Make these and see the remarkable difference. Serve with fresh fruit or jam and yogurt cheese.

If you are using frozen berries, add them while they are still frozen.

1 cup (250 mL) all-purpose flour
3/4 cup (175 mL) whole wheat flour or all-purpose flour
1/3 cup (75 mL) granulated sugar
4 tsp (20 mL) baking powder
2 tbsp (25 mL) grated lemon peel
1/4 tsp (1 mL) salt
1/3 cup (75 mL) butter, cold, cut in pieces
1 cup (250 mL) fresh or frozen blueberries
1 egg
1/2 cup (125 mL) milk
2 tbsp (25 mL) light cream or milk
2 tbsp (25 mL) coarse sugar

1. In a large bowl, combine flours, granulated sugar, baking powder, lemon peel and salt. Cut in butter until it is in tiny bits. Stir in blueberries. (Be gentle with blueberries so they are not crushed.)

2. In a small bowl, combine egg and milk. Add to flour mixture and mix in. Gather dough into a ball and knead everything gently together.

3. Pat or roll dough on a floured work surface until it is approximately 6 inches (15 cm) square. Cut into 9 squares.

4. Transfer scones to a baking sheet lined with parchment paper. Brush with cream and sprinkle with coarse sugar.

5. Bake in a preheated 450 F (230 C) oven for 12 to 15 minutes, or until lightly golden.

Makes 9 scones

Rhubarb Streusel Muffins

Instead of rhubarb you can use fresh or frozen berries or 2 cups (500 mL) chocolate chips.

1 1/2 cups (375 mL) all-purpose flour
1 cup (250 mL) whole wheat flour or all-purpose flour
1 tsp (5 mL) baking powder
1 tsp (5 mL) baking soda
Pinch salt
1 egg
1/3 cup (75 mL) melted butter or vegetable oil
1 cup (250 mL) buttermilk or unflavored yogurt
3/4 cup (175 mL) brown sugar
3 cups (750 mL) fresh or frozen diced rhubarb

Topping
1/4 cup (50 mL) brown sugar
1/4 cup (50 mL) all-purpose flour
1/2 tsp (2 mL) ground cinnamon
1/3 cup (75 mL) large-flake rolled oats
3 tbsp (45 mL) butter, melted

1. In a large bowl, combine flours, baking powder, baking soda and salt.

2. In a separate bowl, combine egg, melted butter, buttermilk and brown sugar. Stir into dry ingredients. Stir in rhubarb just until blended. Scoop batter into 12 nonstick or paper-lined muffin cups. (An ice cream scoop works well for this.)

3. For topping, in a bowl, combine brown sugar, flour, cinnamon, rolled oats and melted butter. Sprinkle over muffins.

4. Bake in a preheated 400 F (200 C) oven for 25 minutes, or until a cake tester comes out clean. Remove muffins from pan and cool on racks.

Makes 12 muffins

Breakfast Salad with Poached Eggs and Smoked Salmon

This is a version of the wonderful bistro salad that combines poached eggs, croutons and bacon bits. In this recipe, instead of the croutons and bacon, I use potatoes and smoked salmon.

The eggs can be poached ahead of time. Count on one or two per person. Immerse them in ice water as soon as they are cooked, drain on a paper towel and trim. Reheat in boiling water for a minute before serving.

1 lb (500 g) baby new potatoes, halved

4 cups (1 L) mixed greens

1 tbsp (15 mL) red wine vinegar

1/2 tsp (2 mL) Dijon or honey-style mustard

1 tsp (5 mL) honey

1/2 tsp (2 mL) salt

3 tbsp (45 mL) olive oil

1 tbsp (15 mL) chopped fresh tarragon, or 1/2 tsp (2 mL) dried

1 tbsp (15 mL) white vinegar

4 or 8 eggs

8 oz (250 g) smoked salmon, sliced

1. Cook potatoes in a pot of boiling salted water until tender, about 20 minutes. Drain well. Cool slightly.

2. Place greens in a large bowl. Add potatoes.

3. In a small bowl, whisk together red wine vinegar, mustard, honey and salt. Whisk in olive oil. Stir in tarragon.

4. Just before serving, fill a deep skillet with water, bring to a boil and add vinegar. Break eggs into a bowl and slip into water one at a time. Cook for 3 to 4 minutes, or until whites are set and yolks are still liquid. Lift eggs out of water with a slotted spoon and drain on paper towels. Trim off any scraggly edges.

5. Toss salad and potatoes with dressing. Divide among four plates. Top each serving with two slices of smoked salmon and one or two eggs. Serve immediately.

Makes 4 servings

Bircher Muesli

Muesli, a raw oatmeal cereal, is one of my favorite breakfasts. Some versions are dry, like granola, and others, like this one, are wet.

I fell in love with muesli when I was traveling in Switzerland (where it was invented at a health clinic). I have tried rich versions that contain whipped cream and leaner versions that include all kinds of grains, but this one is nicely balanced for my taste.

Serve about 1/2 cup (125 mL) per person.

2 cups (500 mL) large-flake
  rolled oats
1/2 cup (125 mL) barley flakes
1/2 cup (125 mL) milk
1 apple, grated (peeled or
  unpeeled)
3/4 cup (175 mL) orange juice
1/4 cup (50 mL) honey
3/4 cup (175 mL) unflavored
  yogurt
2 cups (500 mL) fresh berries

1. In an 8-inch (1.5 L) baking dish, combine oats, barley flakes, milk, apple, orange juice and honey. Cover and refrigerate overnight.
2. Stir in yogurt and berries before serving.

Makes 3 cups (750 mL)

Vegetable and Cheese Galette

There are many open-air markets in Paris, but if you are there on a Sunday morning, don't miss the organic market on Boulevard Raspail. The last time I was there, everyone was eating delicious thick vegetable pancakes, or galettes. Here's how I remember them. (Small ones also make great appetizers.) If you add the cheese, be sure to use a nonstick pan.

1/2 cup (125 mL) small dried
  red lentils
2 cups (500 mL) water
1 cup (250 mL) all-purpose flour
1/2 cup (125 mL) whole wheat
  flour
1 1/2 tsp (7 mL) salt
1 tsp (5 mL) ground cumin
3 eggs
1 cup (250 mL) unflavored yogurt
  or buttermilk
1 cup (250 mL) grated carrots
  (about 2 medium)
1 cup (250 mL) fresh or
  frozen corn kernels
2 tbsp (25 mL) vegetable oil
1 cup (250 mL) grated Swiss
  cheese, optional

1. Rinse lentils and place in a medium saucepan with water. Bring to a boil. Reduce heat and simmer gently, uncovered, for 10 to 15 minutes, or until lentils are completely tender and water has been almost completely absorbed. Cool.

2. Meanwhile, in a medium bowl, combine flours, salt and cumin.

3. In a large bowl, beat eggs lightly with yogurt. Stir in cooled lentils. Stir in flour mixture, carrots and corn. Cover batter and let rest for 30 minutes if you have time.

4. Heat oil in large nonstick skillet on medium-high heat. Stir hot oil into batter.

5. Return pan to heat. Make pancakes one at a time using about 3/4 cup (175 mL) batter for each and spreading it to about 4 to 5 inches (10 to 12 cm) in diameter (or make smaller cakes to serve as appetizers). Cook pancakes for 1 to 2 minutes, or until browned on bottom. Flip. Cook second side for about 1 minute, or until browned. Flip again. Sprinkle pancakes with cheese if using. Cook for 30 seconds longer. Flip and cook for 30 to 60 seconds, or until cheese melts and browns (that's why a nonstick or very well-seasoned pan is a must). Serve pancakes cheese side up.

Makes 6 large galettes or 32 small ones

Southwest Breakfast Wraps

These are fun and have as many variations as an omelette. Use different cheeses, cooked vegetables, and fillings such as smoked salmon, leftover chicken, cooked shrimp, ham or bacon. You can make the wraps ahead, wrap them in foil and reheat in the oven, or you can chill and slice them to make little appetizers.

If you are making several of these at once, wrap the tortillas in foil and heat at 350 F (180 C) for 10 minutes. Mix up a big batch of eggs and use about 1/2 cup (125 mL) beaten egg for each omelette.

2 eggs

1 tbsp (15 mL) water

1 tsp (5 mL) pureed chipotles or
   finely chopped jalapeños

1/2 tsp (2 mL) salt

1 tsp (5 mL) butter or olive oil

1/4 cup (50 mL) grated smoked
   mozzarella or Cheddar cheese

1 tbsp (15 mL) chopped
   fresh cilantro

1 10-inch (25 cm) flour tortilla

1. In a small bowl, beat eggs lightly with water, chipotles and salt.

2. Heat butter in a 10-inch (25 cm) nonstick skillet on medium-high heat. Add eggs and cook for about 1 to 1 1/2 minutes, or until eggs start to set. Tilt pan or lift eggs with spatula so unset egg mixture moves to bottom of pan. Sprinkle eggs with cheese and cilantro and cook for 1 minute longer, just until cheese starts to melt.

3. Heat a separate skillet or grill pan on medium-high heat. Add tortilla and warm for about 10 seconds per side. Place on a plate. Slide omelette onto tortilla and roll up. Cut in half on the diagonal. Eat like a sandwich.

Makes 1 serving

I love all kinds of crêpes and pancakes, whether they are big puffy pancakes baked in the oven, crêpes filled with sweet or savory fillings, rolled pancakes, or my mother's blintzes.

Pancake and Crêpe Tips:

• Pancake batters usually contain baking soda or baking powder or another leavening agent. Crêpe batters are usually very thin.

• For tender crêpes, let the batter rest for 30 to 60 minutes before cooking if you have time. (Do not do this with pancake batter or the baking powder and/or baking soda may lose some of their effectiveness.)

• Pancakes are ready to flip when the tops have lost their sheen. Crêpes are ready to flip when they are brown on the bottom (you should almost be able to see right through them).

• If you are making pancakes containing berries or chocolate chips, sprinkle them onto the half-cooked pancakes just before flipping to cook the second side. There will be less burning, less running, and the chocolate and/or berries are divided more fairly! Be careful when adding chocolate chips, as they burn easily. If you are using frozen berries, add them while they are still frozen.

• Crêpe fillings could include caramelized apples, tomato sauce and grated mozzarella cheese, applesauce and grated Cheddar cheese, orange marmalade or Nutella.

Basic Crêpes

Crêpes are extremely versatile. Fill them with sweet or savory fillings, eat them simply sprinkled with lemon juice and sugar (one of my favorites), or turn them into a spectacular dessert. You can make the batter ahead and keep it in the refrigerator for two to three days in case someone needs a last-minute breakfast, snack or lunch.

Here is my favorite crêpe batter and two great things to do with it—one for children of all ages and one that is distinctly adult.

3 eggs
3/4 cup plus 2 tbsp (225 mL) all-purpose flour
1 1/2 cups (375 mL) milk
1 tbsp (15 mL) granulated sugar
1 tbsp (15 mL) vegetable oil
Pinch salt
1 tsp (5 mL) butter

1. In a blender or food processor, combine eggs, flour, milk, sugar, oil and salt. Process until smooth. If possible, let batter rest, covered, for 30 minutes, or up to overnight in refrigerator.
2. Heat butter in an 8- or 9-inch (20 or 23 cm) nonstick skillet on medium-high heat. When skillet is hot, add about 1/4 cup (50 mL) batter and swirl around bottom of pan. Cook for 1 to 2 minutes, or until browned. Flip crêpe and cook second side for about 1 minute, or until browned. Continue until all batter is used.

Makes 8 to 12 crêpes

Crêpes with Bananas and Chocolate

Slice half a banana over one half of each cooked crêpe. Sprinkle with about 1 tbsp (15 mL) chocolate chips. Fold unfilled side over filled side. As crêpes are filled, place on a baking sheet in a single layer.

When all crêpes are assembled, place in a preheated 300 F (150 C) oven for 15 minutes, or until chocolate melts.

Makes 8 servings

Crêpes Suzette

For sauce, sprinkle 1/2 cup (125 mL) granulated sugar over bottom of a large heavy skillet. Cook on medium-high heat until sugar melts and turns golden. Add 2 tbsp (25 mL) butter and cook until melted. Add 3/4 cup (175 mL) orange juice, 1 tbsp (15 mL) lemon juice, 1 tbsp (15 mL) grated orange peel and 1/4 cup (50 mL) orange liqueur. Bring to a boil.

Add cooked crêpes to pan one at a time. Swish each crêpe in sauce and then fold in quarters. (Push crêpes to side of pan after you fold them.)

Sprinkle crêpes with 2 tbsp (25 mL) brandy or Cognac. Heat brandy for 10 to 20 seconds and ignite using a long match. Serve crêpes after flame dies down.

Makes 6 to 8 servings

Blueberry Flax Pancakes

These pancakes are delicious and healthful. Flax is perishable, so store it in the freezer. Grinding or crushing the seeds releases their healthful properties (buy ground flax or grind it yourself in a small spice or coffee grinder). I like the texture of whole seeds that have been lightly crushed, so I usually include those, too. (If you don't have flax, use 1 1/2 cups/375 mL flour.)

Add the berries to the partially cooked pancakes just before you flip them (if you are using frozen berries, add them while they are still frozen). Serve with maple syrup.

1 1/4 cups (300 mL)
  all-purpose or whole wheat flour
1/2 cup (125 mL) ground
  flax seeds
1 tbsp (15 mL) whole flax seeds,
  lightly crushed
1/4 cup (50 mL) granulated sugar
2 tsp (10 mL) baking powder
1/2 tsp (2 mL) baking soda
1/4 tsp (1 mL) ground cinnamon
Pinch salt
2 eggs
1 1/2 cups (375 mL) buttermilk
4 tbsp (60 mL) melted butter or
  vegetable oil, divided
2 cups (500 mL) fresh or
  frozen blueberries

1. In a bowl, combine flour, ground flax, crushed flax, sugar, baking powder, baking soda, cinnamon and salt.

2. In a large bowl, whisk eggs with buttermilk and 3 tbsp (45 mL) melted butter. Stir in flour mixture. Do not overmix; batter should be a little lumpy.

3. Heat a large nonstick skillet or griddle on medium-high heat. Brush with remaining 1 tbsp (15 mL) melted butter. Drop batter by 1/4 cup (50 mL) measure into pan. Cook for about 2 minutes, or until surface loses its sheen. Drop a few blueberries into each pancake. Flip. Cook second side for about 1 minute. Repeat until all batter is used.

Makes 10 to 12 3-inch (7.5 cm) pancakes

Apple Puff Pancake

This is so easy that it will quickly become a family favorite. I sometimes even make it as a last-minute dessert. Use a firm apple such as Golden Delicious or Fuji.

1/4 cup (50 mL) butter

2 apples, peeled and sliced

1/2 tsp (2 mL) ground cinnamon

3 tbsp (45 mL) brown sugar

3 eggs

1 tbsp (15 mL) granulated sugar

1/2 cup (125 mL) milk

1/2 cup (125 mL) all-purpose flour

2 tbsp (25 mL) icing sugar, sifted

1. Melt butter in a 9- or 10-inch (23 or 25 cm) heavy nonstick ovenproof skillet on medium-high heat. Transfer 2 tbsp (25 mL) melted butter to a blender or food processor.

2. Add apple slices, cinnamon and brown sugar to butter remaining in skillet and cook for 10 minutes, or until apples are tender.

3. Meanwhile, add eggs, granulated sugar, milk and flour to butter in blender. Blend until smooth. Pour over apples in skillet.

4. Bake in a preheated 425 F (220 C) oven for 20 minutes, or until browned and puffed.

5. Shake pan to loosen pancake. Invert onto a serving platter and dust with sifted icing sugar.

Makes 6 servings

Finnish Berry Pancake Roll

Thunder Bay has the largest Finnish population of any city outside Finland, and when I was invited there to teach, my hosts, Betty Carpick and Fern Vezeau, took me on a tour of the Finnish restaurants to compare pancakes. This version, which is perfect for brunch, is adapted from Finnish cook Beatrice Ojakangas. I think it is incredible served with maple syrup, but that is a totally Canadian touch.

You can roll the pancake out of the pan like an omelette (using a spatula), or slide it out of the skillet onto a tea towel or parchment paper and use heatproof rubber gloves to roll it up. Or you can simply cut it into wedges.

1 egg

1 cup (250 mL) milk

1/2 cup (125 mL) all-purpose flour

1/4 cup (50 mL) granulated sugar, divided

Pinch salt

2 tsp (10 mL) butter

1 cup (250 mL) fresh or frozen mixed berries

1 tbsp (15 mL) icing sugar, sifted

1. In a food processor or blender, combine egg, milk, flour, 2 tbsp (25 mL) granulated sugar and salt. Process just until smooth.

2. Melt butter in a 10-inch (25 cm) nonstick ovenproof skillet on medium-high heat. Add batter. Bake in a preheated 350 F (180 C) oven for 25 minutes, or until just set and slightly puffed.

3. Sprinkle pancake with berries and remaining 2 tbsp (25 mL) granulated sugar. Return to oven for 10 minutes, or until pancake is cooked through. Remove from oven and loosen edges of pan.

4. Gently slide pancake out of pan and roll up onto a serving platter. Dust with sifted icing sugar and serve in slices.

Makes 2 to 3 servings

Corn Crêpes with Molten Mozzarella

This is a combination pancake, crêpe and wrap. It makes a great vegetarian brunch or lunch dish. You can make mini versions or cut the larger crêpes in thirds or quarters to serve as appetizers. The filling is also great in quesadillas.

3 cups (750 mL) grated smoked
  mozzarella cheese
  (about 12 oz/375 g)

3/4 cup (175 mL) fresh or frozen
  corn kernels

2 tbsp (25 mL) finely chopped
  cilantro

1 jalapeño, seeded and finely
  chopped, optional

3/4 cup (175 mL) all-purpose flour

1/2 cup (125 mL) yellow cornmeal

3 tbsp (45 mL) granulated sugar

1 tsp (5 mL) ground cumin

1 1/2 tsp (7 mL) salt

3 eggs

1 1/2 cups (375 mL) milk

2 tbsp (25 mL) vegetable oil,
  divided

1. In a bowl, combine cheese, corn, cilantro and jalapeño if using.

2. In a separate bowl, combine flour, cornmeal, sugar, cumin and salt.

3. In a blender or food processor, combine eggs, milk and 1 tbsp (15 mL) oil. Add flour mixture and blend until smooth. If you have time, let batter rest, covered, for 30 minutes.

4. Heat remaining 1 tbsp (15 mL) oil in an 8-inch (20 cm) nonstick skillet on medium heat. Add 1/2 cup (125 mL) batter and cook for 1 to 2 minutes, or until set. Bottom should be lightly browned. Flip crêpe and cook second side for 1 to 2 minutes, or until browned. Flip back again. Sprinkle half of crêpe with cheese mixture. Fold over. Transfer crêpe to a baking sheet.

5. Repeat until all batter is used, placing crêpes on a baking sheet in a single layer as they are ready.

6. Heat crêpes, covered, in a preheated 350 F (180 C) oven for 10 to 15 minutes, or until cheese melts.

Makes 6 servings

Jenny's Challah

My grandmother Jenny Soltz had eleven children. The family was very poor but she kept them in bread all winter by winning first place in the county fair with her amazing challah. The prize was flour.

For the photo, we used two-thirds of the dough and baked it in one pan.

1 tsp (5 mL) granulated sugar

2 cups (500 mL) warm water
  or milk, divided

2 tbsp (25 mL) dry yeast
  (2 packages)

1/2 cup (125 mL) vegetable oil
  or butter, cut in bits

1/2 cup (125 mL) granulated sugar

1 tbsp (15 mL) kosher salt

4 eggs, lightly beaten

6 to 8 cups (1.5 to 2 L) all-purpose
  flour

1 tbsp (15 mL) sesame seeds

1. In a 2-cup (500 mL) measure, dissolve 1 tsp (5 mL) sugar in 1/2 cup (125 mL) warm water (about 110 F/45 C). Sprinkle yeast on top. Let sit for about 10 minutes, or until yeast bubbles up and mixture doubles in volume.

2. Meanwhile, in a bowl, combine remaining 1 1/2 cups (375 mL) warm water, oil, 1/2 cup (125 mL) sugar and salt.

3. Reserve 2 tbsp (25 mL) beaten eggs for glaze and add remaining eggs to liquid. Mixture should be lukewarm. Stir down yeast and add to liquid.

4. Place 6 cups (1.5 L) flour in a large bowl and stir in liquid. This can be done by hand or in a mixer with a dough hook. Stir in enough flour to make a soft dough.

5. Knead dough for about 10 minutes by hand or 5 minutes in a mixer. Add extra flour if dough is sticky. Mixture may need up to 8 cups (2 L) flour or more. (It is always better to have a slightly moist dough than a dry one.)

6. Place dough in an oiled bowl and roll it around. Cover with plastic wrap and a tea towel. Set in a warm place. Let rise until doubled, about 1 hour.

7. Punch dough down and divide in half. Divide each half into three strands and roll into long ropes. Braid three strands together and coil into a round. Place each coil in an oiled or buttered 8-inch (20 cm) springform pan. Cover loosely with oiled plastic wrap and let rise for 1 hour or until doubled in bulk.

8. Brush challahs gently with reserved beaten egg. Sprinkle with sesame seeds. Bake in a preheated 350 F (180 C) oven for 25 to 30 minutes, or until internal temperature reaches 190 F (88 C). (If you make one large challah, bake for 50 to 60 minutes.)

Makes 2 challahs

Sticky Buns

Prepare dough for challah and let rise once. Punch dough down and roll out one-third of dough into a rectangle about 16 x 12 inches (40 x 30 cm). Spread with about 2 tbsp (25 mL) soft butter, and sprinkle with 1 cup (250 mL) brown sugar, 1 tsp (5 mL) ground cinnamon and 1 cup (250 mL) raisins and/or chopped pecans. Roll up tightly lengthwise and cut into 12 pieces.

  Rub a 12- x 8-inch (3 L) baking dish with 2 tbsp (25 mL) additional soft butter and sprinkle with 1/2 cup (125 mL) brown sugar. Place rolls in dish cut side up. Cover with buttered plastic wrap and let rise for 1 hour. Bake at 350 F (180 C) for 35 minutes.

Makes 12 buns

Cookies

Homemade cookies and squares used to be considered snack foods, children's lunch box treats or bake sale items. But now I often serve cookies for dessert. I call them mini desserts. They are perfect after a heavy meal when you don't want to eat a lot but just want something small and sweet. They are also perfect when you want to offer a choice, but it would be overwhelming to prepare a selection of regular desserts.

When I was asked to provide desserts for a fundraiser for the National Ovarian Cancer Association, I brought my mini desserts. I decorated long white platters with vines and strawberries and piled up brownies, blondies, butter tart squares, white chocolate pecan cookies and luscious lemon squares. It was a big hit. Everything looked spectacular, and people could eat as much or as little as they wanted.

Warm White Chocolate Pecan Cookies

I love to have cookies baking in the kitchen while my guests are eating dinner at the table. The aroma of fresh baking wafting through the house is intoxicating. This recipe makes a lot of cookies; roll the dough into logs and freeze them so the cookies can be sliced and baked at dinner time, or whenever you need them (the frozen logs also make great hostess or Christmas gifts).

This is an adaptation of a recipe from pastry chef Jocelyn Skill.

1 1/2 cups (375 mL) butter

1 1/2 cups (375 mL) brown sugar

1 cup (250 mL) granulated sugar

2 eggs

2 tsp (10 mL) vanilla

3 1/2 cups (875 mL) all-purpose
   flour

1 1/2 tsp (7 mL) baking soda

1/2 tsp (2 mL) salt

12 oz (375 g) white chocolate,
   coarsely chopped (about
   2 cups/500 mL)

1 1/2 cups (375 mL) toasted
   pecans, coarsely chopped

1. In a large bowl or in a food processor, cream butter with both sugars until very light. Beat in eggs and vanilla.

2. In a separate bowl, combine flour, baking soda and salt.

3. Stir flour into butter mixture until well mixed. Stir in chocolate and nuts.

4. Shape dough into 4 logs about 1 1/2 inches (4 cm) in diameter and 10 inches (25 cm) long. Wrap each log in waxed paper and freeze for up to 3 months.

5. To bake, cut logs into slices 1/2 inch (1 cm) thick and place a few inches apart on parchment-lined baking sheets. (You should have about 20 cookies per roll.)

6. Bake in a preheated 350 F (180 C) oven for 8 to 10 minutes, or until crispy on the outside but still chewy on the inside. Serve warm or cool on racks.

Makes 80 cookies

Gwen's Almond Haystacks

When my Montreal friend Gwen Berkowitz tells me something is delicious, I always make it right away, as she has incredibly good taste. She seems to have a never-ending supply of wonderful recipes.

If you are making these for Passover, omit the vanilla.

2 egg whites

1/2 cup (125 mL) granulated sugar

1/2 tsp (2 mL) vanilla

3 cups (750 mL) sliced almonds

1. In a large bowl, stir together unbeaten egg whites and sugar (do not whip). Stir in vanilla and almonds.

2. With a teaspoon, drop small mounds of mixture on a parchment-lined baking sheet. Bake in a preheated 350 F (180 C) oven for about 20 minutes, or until golden brown. Turn off oven. Leave cookies in oven with door open for 10 more minutes.

Makes about 30 cookies

Lemon Polenta Biscotti with Apricots and Currants

When I started teaching at Buffalo Mountain Lodge in Banff, master chef Hubert Aumeier was the general manager. He now runs a hotel in Austria, but I still make his recipes all the time. This is one of my favorite biscottis.

1/2 cup (125 mL) butter

3/4 cup (175 mL) granulated sugar

1/2 cup (125 mL) yellow cornmeal

2 eggs, lightly beaten

1/4 cup (50 mL) lemon juice

1 tbsp (15 mL) grated lemon peel

1 tsp (5 mL) vanilla

2 1/4 cups (550 mL) all-purpose
    flour

1 1/2 tsp (7 mL) baking powder

1/4 tsp (1 mL) salt

1 cup (250 mL) currants

1 cup (250 mL) dried apricots,
    diced

1. In a food processor or large bowl, beat butter and sugar until light. Beat in cornmeal. Blend in eggs, lemon juice, lemon peel and vanilla.

2. In a separate bowl, combine flour, baking powder and salt. Mix into butter mixture. Stir in currants and apricots. Refrigerate dough, covered, for 1 hour.

3. With floured hands, shape dough into logs about 3 inches (7.5 cm) wide and 12 inches (30 cm) long. Place each log on a parchment-lined baking sheet (stack two baking sheets together to help prevent burning) and press down slightly.

4. Bake in a preheated 350 F (180 C) oven for 25 to 35 minutes, or until logs have spread and puffed slightly. Remove cookies from oven and cool on pan for 15 minutes. Reduce oven temperature to 325 F (160 C).

5. With a serrated knife, cut logs into slices 1/2 inch (1 cm) thick. Place on baking sheets, cut side down. Return to oven and bake for 10 minutes. Turn cookies and bake for 5 to 10 minutes longer, or until dry and lightly colored. Cool on racks.

Makes 30 cookies

Survival Cookies

For the past two years I have taught cooking classes to heli-hikers at Canadian Mountain Holidays' Valemount Lodge. I am not very athletic (except for my treadmill), so no one could believe it when I actually went heli-hiking. It was a very spiritual experience being up in those mountains. These chewy cookies, from Valemount's Melissa Radcliffe, contain all the ingredients hikers need to keep going.

2 cups (500 mL) butter

1 1/2 cups (375 mL) brown sugar

1 1/4 cups (300 mL) granulated sugar

3 eggs

1 tbsp (15 mL) vanilla

2 1/2 cups (625 mL) all-purpose flour

1 1/4 tsp (6 mL) baking soda

1/2 tsp (2 mL) salt

3 3/4 cups (925 mL) large-flake rolled oats

3/4 cup (175 mL) poppy seeds

1 1/2 cups (375 mL) raw unsalted sunflower seeds

1 1/2 cups (375 mL) pumpkin seeds

2 1/2 cups (625 mL) chopped dates

1. In a food processor or large bowl, cream butter with sugars until light. Add eggs one at a time, beating well after each addition. Blend in vanilla.

2. In a separate bowl, combine flour, baking soda and salt. Stir into batter.

3. By hand, stir in oats, poppy seeds, sunflower seeds, pumpkin seeds and dates.

4. Use 1/4 cup (50 mL) batter for each cookie and place on parchment-lined baking sheets about 2 inches (5 cm) apart. Refrigerate for at least 1 hour.

5. Bake in a preheated 350 F (180 C) oven for about 15 minutes, or until cookies are crisp but still chewy. Cool on racks.

Makes 48 large cookies

Swiss Mountain Shortbread

We have been putting different shortbread cookies in our Christmas gift boxes for many years, but this version is everyone's favorite. The two unusual ingredients are fruit sugar and rice flour. The rice flour makes the cookies very tender; it can be found in supermarkets and health food stores. Fruit sugar is fine granulated sugar. It can be found in the supermarket or you can make your own by whizzing regular sugar in the food processor for about one minute.

2 cups (500 mL) butter

1 cup (250 mL) fruit sugar

3 1/4 cups (800 mL) all-purpose flour

1/2 cup (125 mL) rice flour

12 oz (375 g) milk chocolate Toblerone bars, chopped in chunks

2 tbsp (25 mL) icing sugar

1. In a food processor or large bowl, beat butter until very light. Gradually beat in fruit sugar and continue to beat until sugar is dissolved, about 5 minutes.

2. In a bowl, sift together both flours. Stir into butter mixture and combine well.

3. Save about 50 of the biggest chunks of chocolate (1/2 inch/1 cm) and mix the rest into batter just until combined.

4. Arrange mounds of batter (about 2 tbsp/25 mL each) on parchment-lined baking sheets. Press a chunk of chocolate into each cookie.

5. Bake in a preheated 325 F (160 C) oven for 20 to 25 minutes, or until very lightly browned. Cool on wire racks. Sift icing sugar over cookies.

Makes about 50 cookies

More Than S'mores

These cookies are so easy, yet wherever you take them, people think you are a genius. Keep them in the freezer for emergencies, or at least keep the ingredients on hand in case you need cookies in a hurry.

I like to use milk chocolate in these, but you could also use semisweet or white.

1 lb (500 g) milk chocolate

2 cups (500 mL) miniature marshmallows

2 cups (500 mL) crispy rice cereal

1 cup (250 mL) broken-up Graham wafers

1 cup (250 mL) toasted peanuts

1/2 cup (125 mL) raisins, dried cherries
    or dried cranberries

1 oz (30 g) white or dark chocolate, melted

1. Cut up milk chocolate and heat in a large bowl over a pot of simmering water until just melted. Cool to room temperature.

2. Stir in marshmallows, rice cereal, Graham wafer pieces, peanuts and dried fruit.

3. Spoon mixture onto a waxed paper-lined or parchment-lined baking sheet in mounds, about 2 tbsp (25 mL) each.

4. Drizzle mounds with contrasting melted chocolate. Refrigerate until set.

Makes about 36 cookies

Espresso White Chocolate Blondies

Blondies are brownies made without dark chocolate. For an easy topping, instead of making the caramel, just drizzle each square with a bit of melted white chocolate and place a toasted pecan half on top, or just serve them plain.

To make caramel sauce (great for pouring over ice cream or desserts), make caramel topping, but use 1 cup (250 mL) whipping cream.

/2 cup (125 mL) butter

1 1/4 cups (300 mL) brown sugar

2 tsp (10 mL) instant espresso powder or finely ground instant coffee

1 tsp (5 mL) vanilla

2 eggs

1 cup (250 mL) all-purpose flour

3/4 cup (175 mL) chopped toasted pecans

3/4 cup (175 mL) chopped white chocolate

Caramel Topping

1 cup (250 mL) granulated sugar

3 tbsp (45 mL) cold water

2/3 cup (150 mL) whipping cream

25 pecan halves

1. In a food processor or large bowl, beat butter with brown sugar until light. Beat in espresso powder and vanilla. Add eggs one at a time, beating after each addition.

2. Stir in flour, pecans and chocolate.

3. Spoon batter into a lightly buttered and parchment-lined 8-inch (2 L) square baking pan. Bake in a preheated 350 F (180 C) oven for 30 to 35 minutes, or until brownies are dull on top but center is still a bit soft. Do not overbake. Cool. Cut into squares.

4. Meanwhile, for topping, place granulated sugar and water in a saucepan. Stirring constantly, bring to a boil on medium heat. Brush any crystals down sides of pan with a pastry brush dipped in cold water. Cook, without stirring, until mixture turns a golden caramel color, about 5 to 7 minutes. Watch carefully to make sure caramel does not burn. Remove from heat.

5. Carefully add cream. Mixture will bubble up vigorously. If mixture does not smooth out, return to heat for a few minutes and stir until smooth.

6. Cool sauce until thick and sticky. Drizzle caramel over squares and place a pecan half on each.

Makes 25 squares

Butter Tart Squares

These delicious squares are much easier to make than butter tarts, and you can have just a little piece and not feel guilty. Unless, of course, you then have another little piece. And another . . .

Pastry

1 cup (250 mL) all-purpose flour

1/4 cup (50 mL) granulated sugar

1/2 cup (125 mL) butter, cut in
cubes

Filling

1/4 cup (50 mL) butter

1 cup (250 mL) brown sugar

1/4 cup (50 mL) corn syrup

2 eggs

1 tsp (5 mL) vanilla

1/2 tsp (2 mL) baking powder

4 tsp (20 mL) all-purpose flour

1/2 cup (125 mL) raisins, optional

1. To prepare pastry, combine flour and sugar in a bowl or food processor. Cut in butter until it is in tiny bits.

2. Press flour mixture evenly into bottom of a lightly buttered and parchment-lined 8-inch (2 L) square baking dish, letting paper hang slightly over two sides of pan. Bake in a preheated 350 F (180 C) oven for 20 to 25 minutes, or until lightly browned.

3. Meanwhile, to prepare filling, in a bowl or food processor, cream butter and brown sugar until light and fluffy. Beat in corn syrup and eggs one at a time. Blend in vanilla.

4. In a small bowl, combine baking powder and flour. Stir into filling.

5. Sprinkle raisins, if using, over pastry base. Spread filling over raisins. Bake for 20 to 25 minutes, or until set. Cool. Loosen edges of pastry and lift out of pan. Cut into squares.

Makes 25 squares

Mitchell's Miracle Meringues

Mitchell Davis, director of publications for the Beard House in New York City and author of three cookbooks, is my New York connection and one of my favorite foodie friends. He is smart, remembers everything he learns (he's still young!), and he has an amazing sense of humor.

I adore these billowy, whiter-than-white, crunchy-on-the-outside, marshmallowy-on-the-inside miracle meringues that he made when he taught at my school.

8 egg whites
1 cup (250 mL) granulated sugar
1/2 tsp (2 mL) vanilla (preferably vanilla powder), optional
1 3/4 cups (425 mL) icing sugar, sifted

1. In a large bowl, beat egg whites in electric mixer on medium speed until soft peaks form. Slowly beat in 1 cup (250 mL) granulated sugar. Increase speed to high and continue to beat for about 3 minutes, or until egg whites are thick and shiny. Beat in vanilla if using.
2. Gently fold icing sugar into meringue mixture in three or four additions.
3. Using two spoons, spoon meringue onto parchment-lined baking sheets in 2 tbsp (25 mL) mounds about 1 inch (2.5 cm) apart. (You can also make large meringues using 1 cup/250 mL egg white for each cookie.)
4. Bake in a preheated 150 F (65 C) oven—or as low as your oven goes—for 1 1/2 hours (bake large meringues for about 30 minutes longer). Switch and turn baking sheets in oven halfway through baking time.
5. Turn off oven and leave cookies in oven for a few hours or overnight.

Makes 30 small or 8 large meringues

Luscious Lemon Squares

There are many recipes for lemon squares, but surely these are the best. They look lovely at tea time with a candied violet on top. Although they taste best fresh, I have never turned down one that has been frozen.

Pastry
1 cup (250 mL) all-purpose flour
1/3 cup (75 mL) brown sugar
1/2 cup (125 mL) butter, cut in cubes

Filling
2 eggs
1 cup (250 mL) granulated sugar
2 tbsp (25 mL) all-purpose flour
1/2 tsp (2 mL) baking powder
1/4 cup (50 mL) lemon juice
2 tbsp (25 mL) grated lemon peel

2 tbsp (25 mL) icing sugar, sifted

1. For base, in a bowl or food processor, combine flour and brown sugar. Cut in butter until it is in tiny bits.
2. Press flour mixture evenly into bottom of a lightly buttered and parchment-lined 8-inch (2 L) square baking pan, letting paper hang slightly over two sides of pan. Bake in a preheated 350 F (180 C) oven for 20 to 25 minutes, or until lightly browned.
3. Meanwhile, to prepare filling, beat eggs and granulated sugar in a medium bowl.
4. Combine flour and baking powder in a small bowl and stir into eggs. Stir in lemon juice and peel. Pour over base.
5. Bake for 20 to 25 minutes until set and brown around edges. Cool.
6. Loosen edges of pastry and gently remove from pan, using ends of parchment paper to help you lift. Cut into squares. Dust with sifted icing sugar.

Makes 36 squares

Double Chocolate Brownies

Although we keep trying new brownie recipes just in case, these have been our favorites for years. If people knew how easy it was to make great brownies, they would make them at home all the time. And when you make them yourself, you know you are using the best chocolate.

These brownies can be cut into different shapes with cookie cutters (eat the trimmings). You can also roll small baked brownies or trimmings into balls, dip them in melted chocolate and/or chopped nuts and serve as truffles. Or you can bake the batter in a 9-inch (23 cm) springform pan, cut into wedges and serve with ice cream and chocolate sauce (page 175).

10 oz (300 g) semisweet chocolate, coarsely chopped (about 1 1/2 cups/375 mL)

1 cup (250 mL) butter, cut in pieces

4 eggs

2 cups (500 mL) granulated sugar

2 tsp (10 mL) vanilla

1 cup (250 mL) all-purpose flour

1 tsp (5 mL) baking powder

1 cup (250 mL) chopped toasted pecans

1 cup (250 mL) chopped white chocolate

1. Melt chocolate and butter in a heavy saucepan over low heat. Stir until combined. Cool.

2. In a large bowl, beat eggs until light. Gradually beat in sugar and continue to beat until very thick and pale colored. Add vanilla and melted chocolate/butter. Mix just until blended.

3. In a separate bowl, combine flour and baking powder. Stir into batter. Stir in pecans and white chocolate.

4. Spread batter evenly over a lightly buttered and parchment-lined 13- x 9-inch (3 L) baking pan, allowing paper to hang over two sides slightly. Bake in a preheated 350 F (180 C) oven for 25 to 30 minutes, or until firm on the outside but still moist inside. Do not overbake or brownies will be cake-like instead of chewy.

5. Cool brownies in pan. Loosen brownies from sides of pan and lift out using overhanging parchment paper as handles. Cut into squares.

Makes 32 large squares or 50 medium squares

Rugelach

My aunt, Lil Soles, was famous for her rugelach. They are different from any others I have tasted and literally melt in your mouth.

When people complimented her she would say, "Well, what do you think? I've been making them for almost eighty years." She died at age ninety-five, but her legacy lives on.

My rugelach are very different from Aunt Lil's. They are made with a cream cheese pastry that is easy to work with, so if you are intimidated by pastry, do not worry about this one. In fact, making these will give you pastry confidence.

The big debate is on, though. Do I like mine the best or Aunt Lil's? Make them both and decide. It is a hard job searching for the perfect rugelach.

Bonnie's Rugelach

Pastry

2 cups (500 mL) all-purpose flour

1 cup (250 mL) butter, cold, cut in cubes

1 cup (250 mL) cream cheese, cold, cut in cubes

Filling

1 cup (250 mL) brown sugar

1/2 cup (125 mL) finely chopped toasted pecans

1 tsp (5 mL) ground cinnamon

1/2 cup (125 mL) raspberry jam

Glaze

1 egg, beaten

1/2 cup (125 mL) coarse sugar

1. Place flour in a food processor or large bowl. Cut butter into flour until crumbly. Cut cream cheese into mixture and combine to form a dough. (If you are doing this in a food processor be careful not to overprocess.) Divide dough into 4 balls and wrap in plastic wrap. Refrigerate for a few hours or overnight.

2. In a small bowl, combine brown sugar, pecans and cinnamon.

3. Roll each ball of dough into a 10-inch (25 cm) circle. Spread each circle with about 2 tbsp (25 mL) jam and sprinkle with one-quarter of the brown-sugar mixture.

4. Cut each circle into 12 wedges. Roll up each wedge from the wide end. Place on a parchment-lined baking sheet.

5. Brush each cookie with beaten egg and sprinkle with coarse sugar. Bake in a preheated 350 F (180 C) oven for 20 to 25 minutes, or until browned and crusty. (Cookies can also be frozen baked or unbaked. Bake unbaked cookies directly from the frozen state; they may take a few minutes longer to cook.)

Makes 48 cookies

Aunt Lil's Rugelach

Pastry

1/4 cup (50 mL) warm water

2 tsp (10 mL) granulated sugar

1 tbsp (15 mL) dry yeast (1 package)

2 cups (500 mL) all-purpose flour

Pinch salt

1 cup (250 mL) butter, cold, cut in cubes

2 egg yolks

Filling

2 egg whites

1/2 cup (125 mL) granulated sugar

1/4 cup (50 mL) finely chopped toasted walnuts

1 tsp (5 mL) ground cinnamon

1 cup (250 mL) icing sugar, sifted

1. For pastry, in a 2-cup (500 mL) measure, dissolve sugar in warm water. Sprinkle yeast on top. Let mixture rest for 5 to 10 minutes, or until it bubbles up and doubles in volume.

2. Meanwhile, in a large bowl, combine flour and salt. Using a pastry blender or your fingers, cut in butter until it is in tiny bits.

3. When yeast has risen, stir it down and mix in 2 egg yolks. Stir yeast/egg yolk mixture into flour. Dough will be sticky. Divide dough into four equal parts, pat each piece into a flat disk and wrap in plastic wrap. Refrigerate overnight.

4. For filling, just before baking, beat egg whites in a glass, stainless-steel or copper bowl until light and opaque. Gradually beat in granulated sugar.

5. Combine walnuts and cinnamon in a small bowl.

6. On a lightly floured surface, roll each disk of dough into a 10-inch (25 cm) circle. Cut each circle into 12 wedges. Place 1 tsp (5 mL) egg-white mixture on wide end of each wedge. Sprinkle with 1/2 tsp (2 mL) walnut/cinnamon mixture. Roll each wedge up from wide end and place on an ungreased baking sheet.

7. Bake in a preheated 375 F (190 C) oven for 20 minutes, or until lightly browned.

8. Place icing sugar in a shallow dish. When rugelach come out of oven, roll in icing sugar.

Makes 48 cookies

Aunt Lil's Rugelach Tips

• Rinse the 2-cup (500 mL) measuring cup with warm water before using. This will make it warm and cozy for the yeast.

• Cut the butter into 1-inch (2.5 cm) cubes before cutting it into the flour.

• Take the dough out of the refrigerator 15 minutes before rolling so it won't be too hard to roll.

• Don't overcrowd your oven, or nothing will bake properly. Bake half the cookies while you are rolling out the second half.

• Use an ungreased baking sheet.

Desserts

I love desserts, but I don't eat them too often, and I try not to eat too much. My philosophy is that if you are going to eat dessert, eat only the best, and share it with lots of people. After all, fresh fruit, sorbets, meringues and angel food cake aren't rich at all, and they are also delicious.

Desserts have become big menu items (and profit centers) at restaurants. This ultimate indulgence makes us feel rich and glamorous. But you can have this experience at home, too. Whether you choose a special-celebration dessert or old-fashioned favorite, a delicious dessert prepared with the best and freshest ingredients can be worth the calories, and will make any occasion even more memorable.

Lemon Meringue Pavlova Roll

I have a real soft spot for lemon desserts, and this is my new favorite. Crusty on the outside and billowy soft on the inside, you actually roll the pavlova around a creamy lemon filling. (No one believes me, but trust me, it works!) Garnish with caramel drizzles or serve with marinated strawberries (page 136).

Pavlova

8 egg whites (about 1 cup/250 mL)

1 1/2 cups (375 mL)
   granulated sugar

1 tbsp (15 mL) white vinegar

1 tsp (5 mL) vanilla

2 tbsp (25 mL) cornstarch

1 tbsp (15 mL) icing sugar, sifted

Lemon Curd

1/2 cup (125 mL) lemon juice

1 tbsp (15 mL) grated lemon peel

2/3 cup (150 mL) granulated sugar

4 eggs

1/2 cup (125 mL) whipping cream,
   optional

Orange Caramel Sauce

1/2 cup (125 mL) granulated sugar

2 tbsp (25 mL) water

2 tbsp (25 mL) lemon juice

1/3 cup (75 mL) orange juice

1. For pavlova, in a large bowl, beat egg whites until light. Slowly beat in sugar until whites are stiff and shiny. Beat in vinegar and vanilla. Fold in cornstarch.

2. Spread meringue over a 17- x 11-inch (45 x 29 cm) parchment-lined baking sheet. Bake in a preheated 325 F (160 C) oven for 20 minutes. Cool. Dust top with sifted icing sugar. Run a knife around edge to prevent sticking and then invert onto another piece of parchment.

3. For lemon curd, in a saucepan, combine lemon juice, peel and sugar. Bring to a boil.

4. Beat eggs in a medium bowl. Whisk in hot lemon juice mixture. Return everything to saucepan and cook on medium heat for 3 to 5 minutes, or until thick and bubbling. Strain mixture if you wish, transfer to a clean bowl and chill.

5. Whip cream until light. When lemon mixture is cold, fold in cream.

6. In a small saucepan, combine sugar and water. Cook on medium heat, stirring, just until sugar dissolves. Brush any crystals down sides of pan with a pastry brush dipped in cold water. Cook, without stirring, for 5 to 8 minutes, or until mixture turns a caramel color. Add lemon juice and orange juice. Bring to a boil and stir until smooth.

7. Spread lemon mixture over meringue. Roll up tightly lengthwise. Refrigerate until ready to serve.

8. Cut roll into serving pieces and place on serving plates with sauce.

Makes 8 to 10 servings

Caramel Drizzles

In a small saucepan, combine 1 cup (250 mL) granulated sugar and 3 tbsp (45 mL) water. Cook on medium heat, stirring, until sugar dissolves. Brush any crystals down sides of pan with a pastry brush dipped in cold water. Continue to cook, without stirring, for 5 to 8 minutes, or until mixture turns a caramel color. Transfer to a bowl and cool for a few minutes until caramel thickens slightly.

Carefully set bowl in a larger bowl of hot water to keep caramel liquid but thick. Drizzle caramel in shapes on a buttered sheet of waxed paper and let sit for a few minutes until firm. Carefully remove from paper and decorate dessert just before serving.

Raspberry Meringue Cake

I love the way this tender, berry-laden cake looks in a square pan, but it is easier to remove from the pan and serve if you make it in a springform. (Keep an eye out for the new 9-inch/23 cm square springform pans, which have just become available. The cake will be thinner, but it will still be good.)

Cake

1/3 cup (75 mL) butter,
  at room temperature
1/2 cup (125 mL) granulated sugar
1 egg
1 egg yolk
1 tsp (5 mL) vanilla
1 cup (250 mL) all-purpose flour
1 tsp (5 mL) baking powder
1/4 tsp (1 mL) baking soda
1/2 cup (125 mL) buttermilk or
  unflavored yogurt
1 tbsp (15 mL) grated lemon peel
2 cups (500 mL) fresh raspberries

Meringue

5 egg whites
1 cup (250 mL) granulated sugar

1. To prepare cake, cream butter in a large bowl or mixer. Gradually beat in sugar. Add egg, egg yolk and vanilla and combine thoroughly.

2. In a separate bowl, combine flour, baking powder and baking soda. Stir flour mixture into butter mixture alternately with buttermilk in three or four additions, beginning and ending with flour. Stir in lemon peel.

3. Spoon mixture into a buttered 9-inch (23 cm) springform pan or baking dish and spread evenly. Bake at 350 F (180 C) for 20 to 22 minutes, or until a cake tester inserted in center comes out clean.

4. Sprinkle raspberries over cake.

5. To prepare meringue, beat egg whites in a large bowl until soft peaks form. Slowly beat in sugar. Beat until stiff.

6. Swirl beaten egg whites over cake, making sure meringue touches sides of pan all the way around. Return to oven for 10 to 15 minutes, or until meringue is nicely browned.

Makes 8 servings

Banana and White Chocolate Spring Rolls with Mango Sauce

Of course, these are not spring rolls at all but a wonderful crispy dessert in the shape of spring rolls. I love making them with bananas, but blueberries are also fantastic. (Blueberries are juicier, so if you use them, increase the breadcrumbs to 3/4 cup/175 mL and use about 1 tbsp/15 mL berries per roll.)

You can make the sauce using raspberry sorbet, or serve these with chocolate sauce (page 175), raspberry sauce, caramel sauce (page 158) or melted vanilla ice cream.

8 sheets phyllo pastry

1/3 cup (75 mL) butter, melted

1/2 cup (125 mL) dry
   breadcrumbs

4 bananas (not too ripe), peeled
   and cut in half across and
   lengthwise (16 pieces total)

8 oz (250 g) white chocolate,
   chopped (about 1 cup/250 mL)

Mango Sauce

2 tbsp (25 mL) orange liqueur

2 cups (500 mL) mango sorbet,
   melted

2 tbsp (25 mL) icing sugar, sifted

Fresh mint leaves

1. Arrange one sheet of phyllo on work surface. Cover remaining sheets with plastic wrap and a damp tea towel. Brush phyllo sheet with a little melted butter and sprinkle with some breadcrumbs. Cut phyllo in half crosswise.

2. Place a piece of banana at bottom of each piece of phyllo (make two rolls at a time). Sprinkle each with about 1 tbsp (15 mL) chopped white chocolate. Fold up bottom and fold in sides. Brush with butter and dust with breadcrumbs. Roll up tightly. Brush with butter. Arrange on a parchment-lined baking sheet. Repeat to make 16 rolls. Rolls can be frozen at this point. (You may not need all the chocolate.)

3. For mango sauce, stir liqueur into mango sorbet.

4. Just before serving, bake spring rolls in a preheated 350 F (180 C) oven for 25 to 30 minutes, or until browned and crisp.

5. Drizzle each serving plate with mango sauce. Cut spring rolls in half on the diagonal and arrange two spring rolls (four halves) on each plate. Dust with sifted icing sugar. Garnish each serving with a sprig of mint.

Makes 8 servings

Banana Pecan Cupcakes with Butter Pecan Sauce

My husband, Ray, and my daughter, Anna, both love bananas. But they won't touch them if they are even just a little too ripe, so that's when I start baking. Really ripe bananas add the most flavor and sweetness to cakes and muffins. Mash any leftover bananas and freeze in small plastic bags.

This is a comforting dessert that is also very sophisticated. Serve with the butter pecan sauce and a scoop of vanilla ice cream, or ice the cupcakes with chocolate or vanilla icing (pages 170 and 185) and sprinkle with crushed banana chips. The batter can also be baked in an 8- x 4-inch (1.5 L) loaf pan (bake for 25 to 30 minutes).

2/3 cup (150 mL) mashed
  ripe bananas
1/3 cup (75 mL) sour cream or
  unflavored yogurt
3/4 tsp (4 mL) baking soda
1/3 cup (75 mL) butter
1/2 cup (125 mL) granulated sugar
1/4 cup (50 mL) brown sugar
1 egg
1 tsp (5 mL) vanilla
1 cup (250 mL) all-purpose flour
3/4 tsp (4 mL) baking powder
3/4 cup (175 mL) chopped
  toasted pecans

Butter Pecan Sauce

1 cup (250 mL) granulated sugar
3 tbsp (45 mL) cold water
3/4 cup (175 mL) whipping cream
2 tbsp (25 mL) dark rum,
  or 1/2 tsp (2 mL) vanilla
2 tbsp (25 mL) butter
1/2 cup (125 mL) chopped
  toasted pecans

1. In a small bowl, combine bananas, sour cream and baking soda.

2. In a large bowl or food processor, beat butter with sugars until light. Beat in egg and vanilla.

3. In a separate bowl, combine flour and baking powder. Add to butter mixture alternately with bananas, beginning and ending with flour. (If you do this in a food processor, add all banana mixture to butter mixture and blend. Then briefly blend in flour.) Stir in pecans.

4. Transfer batter to 8 buttered muffin cups. Bake in a preheated 350 F (180 C) oven for 15 to 20 minutes, or until a cake tester comes out clean. Cool for about 10 minutes.

5. Meanwhile, for sauce, combine sugar and cold water in a large saucepan. Bring to a boil on medium-high heat. Stir until sugar dissolves and then do not stir. With a pastry brush dipped in cold water, brush down any sugar crystals that cling to sides of saucepan. Continue to cook, without stirring, for 5 to 6 minutes, or until sugar turns a caramel color. Do not allow mixture to burn.

6. Remove caramel from heat and, standing back, add cream. Mixture will bubble up. Return to a gentle heat. Add rum, butter and pecans. Cook for 1 minute, or until very smooth.

7. To serve, drizzle each cupcake with sauce.

Makes 8 servings

Double Fudge Chocolate Cupcakes

My husband says these cupcakes make him feel as though he is five years old again. They have an amazing deep chocolate flavor, and they freeze well. For an old-fashioned effect, swirl the icing on top of the cupcakes; for a more modern look, pipe it.

You can bake the batter in two deep 9-inch (23 cm) pans and make an old-fashioned layer cake. Bake for 30 to 35 minutes, or until the cake springs back when pressed in the center. We sometimes also make mini cupcakes (you should have about seventy); bake them for 10 to 12 minutes.

1/2 cup (125 mL) cocoa, sifted

2/3 cup (150 mL) chopped
　unsweetened chocolate
　(about 4 oz/125 g)

1 cup (250 mL) boiling water

1 cup (250 mL) butter

1 cup (250 mL) granulated sugar

1 cup (250 mL) brown sugar

3 eggs

1 tbsp (15 mL) vanilla

2 1/2 cups (625 mL)
　all-purpose flour

2 tsp (10 mL) baking powder

1 tsp (5 mL) baking soda

1 cup (250 mL) milk

Chocolate Icing

3/4 cup (175 mL) butter,
　cut in small pieces

12 oz (375 g) semisweet or
　bittersweet chocolate, melted
　and cooled

1/3 cup (75 mL) cocoa, sifted

1 tbsp (15 mL) vanilla

3 cups (750 mL) icing sugar, sifted

1/2 cup (125 mL) milk, approx.

1. Combine cocoa and unsweetened chocolate in a bowl. Pour boiling water over chocolate and let sit for 2 minutes. Whisk until smooth. Cool.

2. In a large bowl or bowl of electric mixer, cream butter with both sugars until very light. Add eggs one at a time. Beat in vanilla and cooled chocolate mixture.

3. In a separate bowl, combine flour, baking powder and baking soda. Add flour to butter mixture alternately with milk in three or four additions, beginning and ending with flour.

4. Fill 24 well-buttered or paper-lined muffin cups. (Fill muffin cups three-quarters full; cupcakes will not rise as much as muffins.) Bake in a preheated 350 F (180 C) oven for 20 to 25 minutes, or until a cake tester comes out clean. Cool on a rack before icing.

5. For icing, in a large bowl or food processor, beat butter until light. Beat in cooled melted chocolate, cocoa and vanilla. Beat in icing sugar. Add milk and beat until very cool and creamy. (Add more milk if necessary for a creamy texture.) If mixture is too warm and thin to spread, set over a bowl of ice; it should thicken very quickly as you beat with a wooden spoon.

6. Swirl or pipe icing on top of cupcakes.

Makes 24 cupcakes

Blueberry Upside-down Cupcakes

Upside-down cake is the essence of a homey dessert. You can use cranberries, raspberries, a mixture of berries or even dried fruit in this recipe. You can also double the recipe and bake the batter in an 8-inch (2 L) square baking dish (bake for 30 to 35 minutes), but the cupcakes are a bit different and they are great for picnics and school lunches. They freeze well, too.

2 tbsp (25 mL) butter, melted

1/3 cup (75 mL) brown sugar

1 cup (250 mL) fresh or
   frozen blueberries

1/4 cup (50 mL) butter,
   at room temperature

1/3 cup (75 mL) granulated sugar

1 egg

1/2 tsp (2 mL) vanilla

3/4 cup (175 mL) all-purpose flour

3/4 tsp (4 mL) baking powder

1/4 tsp (1 mL) baking soda

1/3 cup (75 mL) buttermilk

1. Put melted butter in the bottom of 6 nonstick muffin cups (about 1 tsp/5 mL per cup). Sprinkle about 1 tbsp (15 mL) brown sugar in each cup and pat down. Add about 2 tbsp (25 mL) blueberries.

2. Cream 1/4 cup (50 mL) butter in a large bowl or mixer. Beat in granulated sugar. Beat in egg and vanilla.

3. In a separate bowl, combine flour, baking powder and baking soda. Stir into butter mixture alternately with buttermilk in three additions, beginning and ending with flour.

4. Spoon batter into muffins cups (an ice cream scoop works well). Bake in a preheated 350 F (180 C) oven for 15 to 20 minutes, or until cupcakes spring back when lightly touched in center. Cool on a wire rack for 5 minutes. Invert gently.

Makes 6 cupcakes

Blueberry White Chocolate Clafoutis

Last summer in Vancouver I saw clafoutis on at least eight menus in two days and was reminded how delicious and easy this traditional homestyle French dessert is. (You may wonder why I saw eight dessert menus in two days. Culinary research—what else can I say?)

There are many versions of clafoutis. They can be made with many different fruits. Some are custardy, some cakey, some come with a pastry crust, some without. This one is a combination of my favorites. Not really a cake and not really a custard, it has a texture all its own.

2 cups (500 mL) fresh or
  frozen blueberries
1/2 cup (125 mL) chopped
  white chocolate
1/2 cup (125 mL) butter
3/4 cup (175 mL) granulated sugar
3 eggs
1 tsp (5 mL) vanilla
1 cup (250 mL) all-purpose flour
3/4 cup (175 mL) unflavored
  yogurt
2 tbsp (25 mL) coarse sugar

1. In a small bowl, combine blueberries and chocolate.
2. In a large bowl or food processor, beat butter with sugar. Add eggs and vanilla. Add flour and stir or process in quickly.
3. Fold yogurt into batter with blueberries and chocolate.
4. Spread batter in a lightly buttered 10-inch (25 cm) pie dish or fluted flan pan. Sprinkle with coarse sugar.
5. Bake in a preheated 350 F (180 C) oven for 40 to 45 minutes, or until set.

Makes 8 servings

Double Brûléed Lemon Tart

I love lemon desserts and I love caramel, so this tart is perfect for me. Although this isn't exactly "light," it is far less rich than a traditional crème brûlée but has the same pizzazz.

Although I don't use a blowtorch often, I do keep a small one in the kitchen to caramelize crème brûlées, to brown meringues on pies or cakes or to blacken peppers. The small version is much less unwieldy than a large blowtorch, and it can be used easily and safely if you follow the manufacturer's instructions. You can also place the dessert under a preheated broiler for a minute or two until the top browns, but watch it closely.

This can be baked as individual tarts, which look wonderful, and you don't have to worry about breaking the "glassy" topping to serve it. (To make smaller tarts, roll dough into a fat rope and cut into eight pieces. Roll each piece into a 5-inch/12 cm circle and fit into 3-inch/7.5 cm tart pans with removable bottoms. Bake as for the larger tart. Fill each prebaked tart shell with about 1/3 cup/75 mL filling and top with 1 tbsp/15 mL sugar each time you brûlée.)

The all-purpose pastry can be used in other pies and tarts. This recipe makes enough for one 9- or 10-inch (23 or 25 cm) single-crust pie.

All-Purpose Butter Pastry

1 1/2 cups (375 mL)
   all-purpose flour

Pinch salt

3/4 cup (175 mL) butter,
   cut in cubes

3 tbsp (45 mL) ice water, approx.

Filling

1 cup (250 mL) lemon juice

1 tbsp (15 mL) grated lemon peel

1 cup (250 mL) granulated sugar

1/4 cup (50 mL) butter

6 eggs

Topping

1/2 cup (125 mL) granulated sugar

1. For pastry, in a food processor or large bowl, combine flour and salt. Cut in butter until it is in tiny bits. Sprinkle with ice water and knead dough into a ball. Wrap and refrigerate for 30 minutes.

2. Roll dough into a 12-inch (30 cm) circle to fit a 10-inch (25 cm) tart pan with removable bottom. Press dough into pan and double over pastry around edge. Line pastry with parchment paper, fill with beans, rice or pie weights and bake in a preheated 425 F (220 C) oven for 15 minutes. Remove weights and paper. Reduce heat to 375 F (190 C) and continue to bake pastry for 10 minutes, or until lightly browned.

3. Meanwhile to prepare filling, combine lemon juice, peel, sugar and butter in a saucepan and bring to a boil. Stir well.

4. Beat eggs in a large bowl. Whisk hot mixture into eggs. Return to saucepan and cook for 5 minutes, stirring, until thick. Pour into cooled tart shell and bake in 375 F (190C) oven for 15 minutes. Cool completely and refrigerate (I like to serve this tart cold).

5. Just before serving, sprinkle half of sugar for topping over surface of tart. Using a blowtorch, melt sugar on top of tart until it browns. Move torch in small circles for a more even melt. Allow sugar to set. Sprinkle remaining sugar over tart and repeat. Allow to set for 5 minutes. To serve, use a large chef's knife and cut firmly. (Sugar crust will splinter a little but it looks fantastic anyway.)

Makes 8 servings

Chocolate Pudding with Brownie and Hot Chocolate Sauce

When I was in Spain, I was amazed at how textural the food was, including the desserts. A single dessert dish would combine many different textures, flavors and temperatures. I was inspired, and when I returned home I created this. My kids eat the chocolate pudding on its own.

2 cups (500 mL) milk

3/4 cup (175 mL) granulated sugar

1/4 cup (50 mL) cocoa, sifted

1 tbsp (15 mL) cornstarch

2 eggs

2/3 cup (150 mL) chopped
  semisweet or bittersweet
  chocolate

1 tsp (5 mL) vanilla

8 chocolate brownies (page 161)

Hot Chocolate Sauce

1/2 cup (125 mL) whipping cream

2 tbsp (25 mL) granulated sugar

2 tbsp (25 mL) corn syrup

2/3 cup (150 mL) chopped
  semisweet or bittersweet
  chocolate

2 tsp (10 mL) vanilla

8 small scoops vanilla ice cream

1. In a saucepan, bring milk to a boil. Turn off heat.

2. Meanwhile, in a small bowl, combine sugar, cocoa and cornstarch.

3. In a large bowl, beat eggs. Whisk in sugar mixture. Whisk in warm milk. Return mixture to saucepan. Cook gently for 5 to 8 minutes, or until mixture comes to a boil and thickens. Remove from heat. Add chopped chocolate and stir until melted. Stir in vanilla. For the smoothest texture, strain mixture through a sieve.

4. Cut brownies to fit eight 6-oz (175 mL) ramekins or dessert bowls. Pour chocolate mixture over brownies.

5. For chocolate sauce, in a small saucepan, combine cream, sugar and corn syrup. Bring to a boil. Add chocolate and stir until smooth. Add vanilla.

6. Place a scoop of ice cream on each dessert and spoon hot chocolate sauce on top.

Makes 8 servings

Crème Caramel

In Spain this dessert is called a flan, and it is the national dessert. You can also make it with a layer of apples. Simply sauté two sliced apples in a little butter and place on top of the caramel before you add the custard.

1 cup (250 mL) granulated sugar, divided

2 tbsp (25 mL) water

1 1/2 cups (375 mL) milk

1 1/2 cups (375 mL) light cream

6 egg yolks

3 eggs

1 tsp (5 mL) vanilla

1. Fill a roasting pan half full of hot water. Place in a 350 F (180 C) oven to heat water while preparing custard.

2. For caramel, stir 1/2 cup (125 mL) sugar and water together in a large saucepan on medium-high heat. When sugar is dissolved, stop stirring and cook for 5 to 6 minutes, or until mixture turns to caramel. While it is cooking, brush any undissolved crystals of sugar down sides of saucepan with a pastry brush dipped in cold water. When sugar is a deep golden brown, pour it into a 8- x 4-inch (1.5 L) loaf pan.

3. For custard, heat milk and cream in a saucepan on medium-low heat just until hot.

4. In a large bowl, whisk egg yolks and whole eggs with remaining 1/2 cup (125 mL) sugar. Pour in hot liquid gradually, beating well. Add vanilla.

5. Strain custard over caramel in loaf pan. Place loaf pan in roasting pan of hot water in oven. Bake for 40 to 45 minutes, or until custard is set.

6. Cool custard and refrigerate until cold. To unmold, run a knife around edge of pan. Invert onto a serving plate that has a slight lip to catch caramel. If any caramel sticks to pan, heat it and pour over custard. Serve in slices.

Makes 6 to 8 servings

Old-fashioned Rice Pudding

When I first started my cooking school, I gave out a rice pudding recipe on the radio, and there was such a big response that the station had to change its policy; after that, people had to send in a stamped self-addressed envelope if they wanted a copy of a recipe.

This pudding and the response to it haven't changed much over the years; it's still one of my favorites.

1/2 cup (125 mL) uncooked
    short-grain rice
1 cup (250 mL) boiling water
1/3 cup (75 mL) granulated sugar
1 tsp (5 mL) cornstarch
5 cups (1.25 L) milk
1/3 cup (75 mL) raisins, optional
2 egg yolks, optional
1 tsp (5 mL) vanilla
1 tbsp (15 mL) ground cinnamon

1. Place rice and boiling water in a large saucepan. Bring to a boil. Reduce heat and cook gently, covered, for 8 to 10 minutes, or until rice has absorbed water.

2. Meanwhile, in a small bowl, combine sugar and cornstarch. Whisk in 1 cup (250 mL) milk. Add mixture to rice along with remaining milk. Add raisins if using.

3. Bring pudding to a boil. Partially cover and cook gently for 45 to 60 minutes, stirring occasionally, until very creamy and thick. (If the heat is too low the pudding will take forever to thicken, but if it is too high it will boil over. It is best to stay on the low side, but I promise it will thicken eventually.)

4. Stir in egg yolks if using. Cook gently for 1 minute. Stir in vanilla. Transfer to a serving bowl or individual bowls and dust with cinnamon.

Makes 8 servings

Chocolate Soufflé Roulade with Coffee Caramel Cream

My kids have always been very selective eaters, so when I brought this cake home for the first time and they said those magic words—"Mommy, this is perfect!"—I was in heaven. I would have preferred them to be as enthusiastic about a main course, but sometimes parents can't be picky.

The first time you make a rolled cake, you wonder how it will ever roll up, but don't worry. We love to prepare this in participation classes, because afterwards everyone has the confidence to make it at home.

This is a special-occasion cake. It is dramatic and delicious. Decorate it with strawberries, slices of star fruit, icing sugar and sprigs of mint.

6 eggs, separated

3/4 cup (175 mL) granulated sugar, divided

1/4 cup (50 mL) cocoa, sifted

2 oz (60 g) bittersweet or semisweet chocolate, melted and cooled

1 tsp (5 mL) vanilla

2 tbsp (25 mL) icing sugar, sifted

Coffee Caramel Cream

3/4 cup (175 mL) whipping cream

2 tbsp (25 mL) icing sugar, sifted

1 tsp (5 mL) instant espresso powder or finely ground instant coffee

1/2 cup (125 mL) chopped chocolate-coated caramel bars (2 39 g Skor bars)

Chocolate Mocha Sauce

2/3 cup (150 mL) chopped bittersweet or semisweet chocolate

1/2 cup (125 mL) whipping cream

2 tbsp (25 mL) strong coffee

1. Butter a 15- x 10-inch (40 x 25 cm) jellyroll pan. Line with parchment paper, butter again and dust lightly with flour.

2. In a large bowl, beat egg yolks and 1/2 cup (125 mL) granulated sugar until light. Beat in cocoa, melted chocolate and vanilla.

3. In a separate large bowl, beat egg whites until light. Slowly beat in remaining 1/4 cup (50 mL) granulated sugar. Continue beating until whites are firm. Stir one-quarter of whites into chocolate mixture. Fold in remaining whites.

4. Spread batter evenly over prepared pan. Bake in a preheated 350 F (180 C) oven for 12 to 14 minutes, or until puffed and firm to touch. Cool in pan for at least 10 minutes. Dust cake with sifted icing sugar. Loosen cake from pan and invert onto a tea towel. Cool completely.

5. Meanwhile, for filling, whip cream in a large bowl. Beat in icing sugar and espresso powder. Stir in chocolate pieces.

6. Spread filling over cake. Roll up cake lengthwise or widthwise. (Don't worry if cake cracks a little as you roll; it will still look and taste great.) Transfer to a platter. Slice on the diagonal.

7. For sauce, combine chocolate, whipping cream and coffee in a small saucepan and heat gently until melted and smooth. Cool to room temperature. Drizzle sauce over each piece of cake.

Makes 8 servings

Apple Desserts

My husband, Ray, loves apple desserts. So my files are always bulging with apple recipes, from old family standbys like my mother's apple crisp to cakes, mini strudels and flans. I especially love desserts

that combine apples with my personal favorite flavor, caramel.

These days we have so many cooking and eating apples to choose from. I like to cook with a firm apple such as Golden Delicious, Spy, Fuji or Braeburn, but when I want my apple crisp to taste just like my mother's, I use McIntosh, even though they tend to lose their shape when cooked.

Here are two of my favorite apple recipes—my mother's apple crisp and these cute little strudels (by making small rolls I can bake what I need and freeze the rest unbaked; the frozen rolls can then be baked right from the frozen state). The strudels can also be served in small pieces like cookies.

I serve both these desserts with ice cream and sometimes even with a caramel sauce (page 158).

Mini Apple Strudels

4 apples, peeled, cored and chopped

1/2 cup (125 mL) brown sugar

1 tsp (5 mL) ground cinnamon

2/3 cup (150 mL) dry breadcrumbs, divided

1/4 cup (50 mL) butter, melted

2 tbsp (25 mL) water

2 tbsp (25 mL) granulated sugar

12 sheets phyllo pastry

1. In a large bowl, combine apples, brown sugar, cinnamon and 1/2 cup (125 mL) breadcrumbs.

2. Combine melted butter and water in a small bowl. Combine remaining 2 tbsp (25 mL) breadcrumbs and granulated sugar in another bowl.

3. Arrange one sheet of phyllo on work surface. Cover remaining sheets with plastic wrap and a damp tea towel. Brush phyllo with butter/water mixture and sprinkle with crumb mixture. Repeat so that you have 3 layers.

4. Spoon one quarter of apple mixture along long edge of pastry. Roll up tightly and transfer to a parchment-lined baking sheet. Repeat to make 4 rolls.

5. Cut slits through top layers of pastry (so cutting and serving will be easier). Brush tops of strudels with any extra butter mixture.

6. Bake in a preheated 375 F (190 C) oven for 30 to 35 minutes, or until apples are very tender and pastry is brown and flaky. Serve warm or cold.

Makes 8 to 10 servings

Ruthie's Apple Crisp

6 apples, peeled, cored and sliced

1 1/2 cups (375 mL) all-purpose flour

1 1/2 cups (375 mL) granulated sugar

3/4 cup (175 mL) butter, cold, cut in small pieces

1. Spread apples over bottom of a buttered 13 x 9-inch (3 L) baking dish.

2. In a large bowl, combine flour and sugar. Rub butter in with your fingers until it is in tiny bits.

3. Sprinkle flour mixture over apples. Bake in a preheated 375 F (190 C) oven for 1 to 1 1/2 hours, or until topping is browned and crisp and apples are very tender. If crisp starts browning too much, reduce heat to 350 F (180 C).

Makes 8 servings

Homestyle Tarte Tatin

Tarte tatin is a wonderful upside-down caramelized apple pie. This version is very easy compared to others, and it tastes amazing. For a more perfect look you can rearrange the cooked apples in a spiral pattern before topping them with the pastry, but I never bother.

It may look as though you have too many apples, but they will cook down, so do not worry. Serve plain or with vanilla ice cream.

3/4 cup (175 mL) granulated sugar

1/4 cup (60 mL) butter

10 apples, peeled, cored and
  sliced (about 5 lb/2.5 kg)

1 recipe all-purpose butter pastry
  (page 174) or
  1/2 recipe homemade puff pastry
  (page 4), cold

1 egg, beaten

2 tbsp (25 mL) granulated sugar

1. Sprinkle 3/4 cup (175 mL) sugar over bottom of a 10- or 12-inch (25 or 30 cm) nonstick ovenproof skillet. Cook on medium-high heat until sugar melts and turns golden brown, about 3 to 5 minutes. Do not stir once sugar has dissolved. Add butter and melt.

2. Add apples and bring to a boil. Cook for 10 to 15 minutes, or until apples are tender and almost all liquid has evaporated. Do not stir very much or apples may break. Liquid in pan should be very syrupy. Cool to room temperature.

3. Roll pastry into an 11- or 13-inch (28 or 32 cm) circle. Place over apples. Cut out a few steam slits and tuck edges of pastry inside pan.

4. Brush pastry with egg and sprinkle with 2 tbsp (25 mL) sugar. Bake in a preheated 400 F (200 C) oven for 40 to 45 minutes, or until browned.

5. While pie is hot, run a knife around inside edge of pastry and invert onto a large serving plate.

Makes one 10- or 12-inch (25 or 30 cm) tart

Ruthie's Cheesecake

Big cheesecakes have gone in and out of style, and now they are popular once again. But my mother made little cheesecake squares, which have always been in style.

It is hard to know exactly when to serve large cheesecakes (they are really heavy after a big meal), but these little squares are always good—at tea time, for a snack, on a dessert platter or, as I love them, for breakfast. I like them plain, but you could also top them with sliced mango or fresh berries.

Crust

1 1/2 cups (375 mL)
  Graham wafer crumbs
2 tbsp (25 mL) brown sugar
1/3 cup (75 mL) butter, melted

Filling

1 lb (500 g) cream cheese
1/2 cup (125 mL) granulated sugar
2 eggs
1 tsp (5 mL) vanilla

Topping

1 1/4 cups (300 mL) sour cream
2 tbsp (25 mL) granulated sugar
1/2 tsp (2 mL) vanilla

1. For crust, combine Graham crumbs, sugar and melted butter in a bowl. Press into an 8-inch (2 L) square baking dish.

2. For filling, beat cream cheese with sugar until light. Beat in eggs and vanilla until smooth. Pour over crust. Bake in a preheated 350 F (180 C) oven for 35 minutes, or until set. (Filling should not be runny, but do not overbake.)

3. Meanwhile, to prepare topping, combine sour cream, sugar and vanilla in a small bowl. Spread over hot cheesecake and return to oven for 5 minutes. Cool completely. Refrigerate until firm. Cut into squares.

Makes about 25 squares

White on White Birthday Cake

Whenever it is someone's birthday at the cooking school, we always make a special cake. But all we really want is a plain white cake with plain white icing—like the kind you can buy at the supermarket, but better.

Here it is. Sometimes we bake cupcakes. The recipe makes about two dozen regular cupcakes or seventy mini cupcakes; bake them for 15 to 20 minutes. Decorate the cake or cupcakes with colored sugar, dragees or white chocolate curls.

Cake

1 cup (250 mL) butter,
  at room temperature

1 3/4 cups (425 mL)
  granulated sugar

6 egg whites

2 tsp (10 mL) vanilla

3 cups (750 mL) all-purpose flour

1 tbsp (15 mL) baking powder

1 1/2 cups (375 mL) milk

Vanilla Icing

1 cup (250 mL) butter,
  at room temperature

6 cups (1.5 L) icing sugar, sifted

1/3 cup (75 mL) milk, approx.

2 tsp (10 mL) vanilla

2 oz (60 g) white chocolate,
  melted, optional

Luscious Lemon Cupcakes

Add 1 tbsp (15 mL) grated lemon peel to cake batter. Use half milk and half lemon juice in icing. Bake batter as 24 cupcakes. With melon baller, scoop spoonful of cake out of top of each cupcake and fill with lemon curd (page 166). Pipe icing on cupcakes.

1. To make cake, in a large bowl or electric mixer, cream butter and sugar until very light. Beat in egg whites two at a time, beating thoroughly after each addition. Beat in vanilla.

2. In a separate bowl, sift together flour and baking powder. If you have been using a mixer, switch to a wooden spoon and blend flour into butter mixture alternately with milk in three additions, beginning and ending with flour. Do not overmix.

3. Divide batter between two 9-inch (23 cm) square or round cake pans that have been buttered and lined with parchment paper. Bake in a preheated 350 F (180 C) oven for 25 to 30 minutes, or until a cake tester comes out clean when inserted in center. Cool in pans for 10 minutes and then invert onto racks to cool completely.

4. For icing, in a large bowl, beat butter until light. Gradually beat in about 4 cups (1 L) icing sugar. Beat in milk and vanilla. Gradually beat in remaining icing sugar. Cover icing tightly with plastic wrap if you are not using it right away (you may have to beat in a bit more milk if you make the icing ahead and it thickens).

5. Place one layer of cake, top side down, on serving platter. Spread with about 1 cup (250 mL) icing. Place second layer of cake on first layer, top side up. Spread with icing. Place any extra icing in a piping tube with a small star tip and pipe rosettes around cake.

6. Place melted white chocolate in a squeeze bottle and write Happy Birthday on cake if you wish.

Makes one 9-inch (23 cm) two-layer cake

Strawberry Mousse Angel Food Cake
This special-occasion cake is a dream. My friend Susan Devins could not celebrate a birthday without it. The recipe comes from her mother-in-law, Bertie Devins, and they serve it at all family birthdays. It also makes a perfect summer dessert covered with mixed berries.

I love homemade angel food cake. It is virtually fat free and tastes wonderful served plain or with marinated strawberries (page 136).

You can also serve the strawberry mousse on its own with fresh sliced strawberries in tall parfait glasses or wine goblets. (I have started collecting pressed glass goblets, and the mousse looks incredible served in them.)

For a lighter version of the mousse, use yogurt cheese (page 23) instead of whipping cream.

Cake
1 1/2 cups (375 mL)
   granulated sugar, divided
1 cup (250 mL)
   cake-and-pastry flour
1 1/2 cups (375 mL) egg whites
   (about 12)
1 tsp (5 mL) cream of tartar
Pinch salt
1 tsp (5 mL) vanilla
1 tbsp (15 mL) grated lemon peel

Strawberry Mousse
1 envelope unflavored gelatin
2 tbsp (25 mL) cold water
1 10-oz (300 g) package frozen
   strawberries in syrup, defrosted
1/4 cup (50 mL) granulated sugar
1 tsp (5 mL) vanilla
2 cups (500 mL) whipping cream

4 cups (1 L) fresh strawberries or
   mixed fresh berries

1. To make cake, in a bowl, sift 1/2 cup (125 mL) sugar with flour.

2. Place egg whites in large bowl of electric mixer with cream of tartar and salt. Heat a few cups of water in a medium saucepan and place bowl of egg whites over water. Stir egg whites until they feel a little warm. This takes 3 to 5 minutes. Immediately start beating egg whites with mixer and gradually beat in remaining 1 cup (250 mL) sugar.

3. Beat in vanilla and lemon peel. Gently fold flour mixture into egg whites in three additions.

4. Spoon mixture into an ungreased 10-inch (4 L) tube pan. Bake in a preheated 350 F (180 C) oven for 40 to 45 minutes, or until a cake tester comes out clean. Turn cake upside-down on a rack and cool cake in pan. To remove cake from pan, use a thin knife to loosen sides. Remove tube and run a knife between top of cake and pan to remove rest of pan.

5. Meanwhile, to make mousse, in a small saucepan, sprinkle gelatin over cold water and let stand for 5 minutes to soften. Warm gently to dissolve.

6. Place frozen berries with juices in another small saucepan with sugar and bring to a boil. Cook gently for 10 minutes. Whisk in dissolved gelatin and vanilla. Cool in a bowl set over a larger bowl filled with ice and water until mixture is cool and syrupy.

7. In a bowl, whip cream to soft peaks. Gently fold into cool gelatin mixture. Chill until spreadable but not set.

8. Cut cake in half crosswise. Place base on a cake plate and spread with 1 1/2 cups (375 mL) mousse. Top with top half of cake. Swirl mousse over top and sides. Sprinkle fresh berries on top and around base.

Makes 12 to 16 servings

Kitchen Gadgets

Years ago I did a radio show with Peter Gzowski on CBC's *Morningside*. They told me to bring my favorite kitchen gadget. I was hysterical with indecision, because I had so many favorites. At the time I was able to narrow it down to three: my tongs, my all-time favorite pepper mill and my garlic press. I finally decided on the pepper mill, but to this day I feel badly for my tongs and my garlic press.

There are so many kitchen gadgets available now that you practically need a coach to tell you which ones are worthwhile.

Here are my top ten:

1. Pepper Mill

A good pepper mill is a necessity. Freshly ground pepper makes a huge difference to your cooking. There are many pepper mills on the market, but I found my favorite about twenty years ago, when I took a group to New York for cooking classes at the Peter Kump School of Cooking. It is called the Peppermate, and over the years we've sold thousands. Here's how Peter Gzowski described it on his radio show: It holds a lot of pepper. You can adjust the grind. The top simply lifts off, so you do not have to be a mechanical engineer to open it. Most important, it collects the pepper in a little container at the bottom, so you can see how much you have. Brilliant.

2. Tongs

I cannot cook without tongs; they are an extension of my hand. I use tongs for turning meat without piercing it and for transferring food. I even use them at the table to serve salads, pasta and vegetables. I prefer the practical-looking chef-style tongs with the rounded ends (not the ones with the little hands or forks at the ends).

3. Garlic Press

The Zyliss garlic press has stood the test of time. I have had mine for about thirty years, and other people have told me they have had theirs even longer. I use a garlic press to mince garlic for dips, salad dressings and marinades. (If I am going to sauté garlic, I chop it, as the pureed garlic can stick and burn in the pan.)

4. Digital Meat Thermometer

The new digital meat thermometers are incredible. The probe goes into the meat and you can read the temperature without opening the oven door. Be sure the probe is inserted in the muscle of the meat and does not touch bone, skin, fat or, of course, the bottom of the pan. You can also insert the thermometer for an instant read when you think the meat is done.

I even use the thermometer for bread making—to make sure the water for the yeast is the right temperature (110 F/45 C) and to see whether the bread is baked (the internal temperature should be 190 F/88 C)—and for testing cakes (bake to 185 F/85 C).

5. Grill Pan

This is the pan I never learned about in chef training. It is very heavy and has ridges in the bottom so the food sits on top. It gives food those sexy grill marks that make it look as if it has been cooked on the barbecue. I use the grill pan for steaks, chops, boneless skinless chicken breasts, fish steaks or fillets, vegetables and even tofu. Of course, the pan does not make things taste as if the flames have actually touched your food, but in the winter or when you are in a hurry, it can't be beat for fast, low-fat cooking. I have to admit I like a heavy nonstick pan because it is much easier to clean, but a cast-iron one is great if it has been well seasoned, and you'll probably never have to replace it.

6. Food Mill

Jacques Pépin often used the food mill when he taught at my school.

He jokingly called it the original food processor, and that's a good description. But unlike a food processor, which processes food again and again, the food mill only purees food once, so it is perfect for things like mashed potatoes. It also strains, so it will remove the seeds at the same time that it purees a raspberry sauce, and it will remove the seeds and skins when you are making applesauce.

7. Kitchen Scale

With metric measures being used in schools, and recipes coming in from around the world (many recipes, for example, list flour and other ingredients by weight, not volume), it is becoming more and more important to have a good scale with metric and imperial measures.

8. Microplane Grater

This gadget has reinvented graters. I first saw one when I was cooking at a food festival in Vermont. It was part of the equipment they supplied to visiting chefs, and I was in awe. The microplane grater was originally a rasp used in woodworking, but it has found a permanent home in the kitchen. It works for grating lemon, lime and orange peel, ginger, chocolate for cappuccinos, nutmeg and fresh horseradish. It used to come

only in a long skinny shape, but now there are all kinds of fancier ones.

9. Silpats and Parchment Paper

Silpats are reusable lining sheets that prevent food from sticking. They have been used in professional kitchens for years and are now available to home bakers in all sizes and shapes—to fit everything from baking sheets and cake pans to muffin pans. They are expensive, but if you use them often, they are well worth the cost.

I also use plenty of parchment paper (baking paper). Though Silpats are great, I like to be able to throw away the paper after roasting a chicken or something gooey. I also use parchment paper to wrap things and to line serving platters and bread baskets.

10. Oven Mitts

We have been waiting a long time for good oven mitts—the kind that you do not have to replace because they burn up! Finally, we found them. They look as if they are made out of wetsuit material and are black and very sexy. Expensive, but so worth it.

Index